MORNING COMES AND ALSO THE NIGHT

By the same author

*Non-fiction*
THE LIVING DESERT
THE GREEN GUIDE TO THE EMIRATES
WILD ABOUT CATS
WILD ABOUT REPTILES (with Bish Brown)
ANNOTATED CHECKLIST OF THE PLANTS OF THE UAE
WORKING FOR WILDLIFE
WILD ABOUT MAMMALS
THE COMPREHENSIVE GUIDE TO THE WILDFLOWERS OF THE UAE

*Children's fiction*
HAYAT THE ARABIAN LEOPARD
YAWI THE WILDCAT
DENIS THE DUGONG
SOPHIE THE SANDFOX

*Memoir*
FAT LEGS DON'T MATTER

# Morning Comes and Also the Night

A STORY OF COURAGE AND SURVIVAL
IN JAPANESE INTERNMENT CAMPS
OF NORTH SUMATRA

## Marijcke Jongbloed

MOSAÏQUEPRESS

Published by
MOSAÏQUE PRESS

Registered office:
70 Priory Road
Kenilworth, Warwickshire
CV8 1LQ
www.mosaïquepress.co.uk

Copyright © 2010 Marijcke Jongbloed

All rights reserved. No part of this publication may be reproduced or utilised in any form or by any means, electronic or mechanical, including photocopying, recording or by any information storage and retrieval system without the permission in writing of Mosaïque Press.

Printed in the UK.

ISBN 978-1-906852-03-0

*For Peter*

He called to me... Watchman, what of the night?

Watchman, what of the night?

The watchman said, The morning comes, and also the night.

ISAIAH 21:11-12A

**CONTENTS**

| | |
|---|---|
| Acknowledgements | 11 |
| Maps | 13 |
| Notes on the text | 15 |
| Introduction: A voice from the past | 17 |

| | | | |
|---|---|---|---|
| 1 | – | Equals and opposites | 25 |
| 2 | – | Eastward | 35 |
| 3 | – | World at war | 45 |
| 4 | – | The Japanese occupation | 53 |
| 5 | – | First taste of captivity | 61 |
| 6 | – | Life in Poeloe Brayan | 67 |
| 7 | – | Terror and tedium | 77 |
| 8 | – | Even now, new life | 89 |
| 9 | – | 'Give me strength' | 99 |
| 10 | – | Candles for Christmas | 119 |
| 11 | – | 1944 – A brave new year | 133 |
| 12 | – | The last letters | 151 |
| 13 | – | More alone than ever | 167 |
| 14 | – | Death camp | 183 |
| 15 | – | Turning tides | 195 |
| 16 | – | 'Buried alive' | 209 |
| 17 | – | A double celebration | 221 |

| | | |
|---|---|---|
| 18 – | The aftermath | 229 |
| 19 – | Coming home to chaos | 235 |
| 20 – | After effects | 245 |
| | Appendix A: Enigmatic Japanese | 251 |
| | Appendix B: The poetry | 255 |
| | Glossary | 262 |
| | Sources and selected bibliography | 265 |

## ACKNOWLEDGEMENTS

WRITING THIS BOOK was an adventure – first there was curiosity, then discovery, then came hardship and perseverance, and all the time we came closer to the goal – getting the story out around the sixty-fifth anniversary of the end of the Pacific war.

Like most adventures, this one involved many people to whom I am grateful. I was pleasantly surprised by the generosity of Bert Oudenhoven of the Foundation North Sumatra Documentation who not only allowed me to use text and pictures from the books of the series *North Sumatra during the war (Noord Sumatra in Oorlogstijd)* but also consulted friends to provide me with some unpublished data.

I encountered the same generous attitude in Robert Rouveroy who gave me permission to use his website text and pictures a few months before he passed away in November 2009. Rudy Kousbroek allowed me to quote from his book *Return to the country of origin (Terugkeer naar Negri pan Erkoms)* only a few days before he, too, passed away during Easter 2010. I feel especially grateful to Peng ten Velde, who gave me interesting details about my father's life during the last year of internment in the Si Rengo Rengo camp – a period about which I did not have much information. The Museon in The Hague gave permission to use some of their published drawings and sent high resolution images of the ones I chose.

Every effort has been made to contact copyright holders for their permission to quote from long out-of-print material. In this context I would especially like to mention Ann Jacobs, from whose book *Ontwortelden* I quoted a long section in translation. I would be pleased to hear from her or her publisher so that proper credit can be included in future editions of this book.

My writing buddy P K Allen and my friends Lyn Hicks, Gerard and Pollyanna Nienhuis read the early versions and made helpful suggestions. They will not recognise the text as it finally turned out. My friends Liesbeth and Luc de Regt read the final version and gave their helpful opinion.

I received a lot of encouragement from old friends who had also been through the camp experience, Liesbeth de Regt and Carien Louwerier. They guessed correctly that the writing of and research for the story was quite difficult at times.

The fun part of creating this book was finding the photographs to illustrate the text. I owe the best ones to my brother, who dug through the mountains of stuff in his attic to find the albums with the pre-war photographs. It is a pity that even more photos could not be used.

I owe this final version to my friend and editor Chuck Grieve. At times we did not see eye to eye about style, but I knew he had just one goal: to create a story that would interest people and keep them reading. I learned a lot.

Last but not least I need to mention Troefke. ("Of course," people who know me will say, "we wondered when she'd get around to mentioning her dog!") It would have been difficult to keep a fresh mind if she had not cajoled me into interrupting the intense involvement in war events with several walks a day to enjoy the beautiful French countryside.

MJ

Rimons, 2010

MAPS – 13

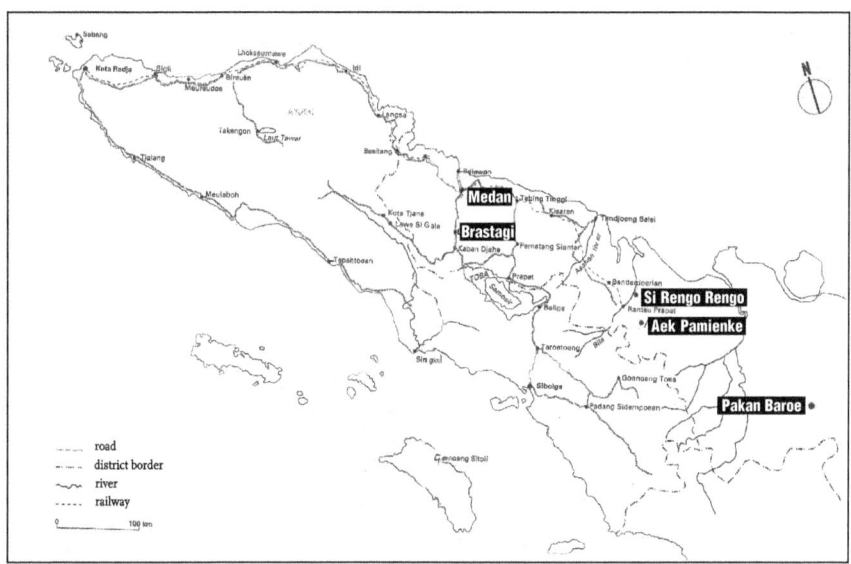

North Sumatra, with detainment camps mentioned in the text highlighted.

The south-western rim of South East Asia, with North Sumatra highlighted.

## NOTES ON THE TEXT

IN THIS BOOK, the spelling of place names has been maintained as it was in the 1940s to give a flavour of the period. Sometimes modern names have been provided in brackets, e.g. Atjeh (Aceh). In addition, a complete glossary of foreign words is found on page 262. Most of the time the meaning of these words can be deduced from the surrounding text.

The Dutch living in the Indies used many Malay words in their daily language, which is what they spoke at home with the servants, or outside when they visited *kampongs* or *pasars*. Many local people also spoke Dutch quite well, but preferred not to. It led to amusing exchanges.

My mother told me a story about an acquaintance of hers who used to say "*Buka tjelana*" to her servant when she wanted him to open the window. Though in fact what she was saying was "Open your pants," he faithfully opened the window (*djendela*) every time!

There were as many languages in the Indies archipelago as there were tribes, and Malay had become a *lingua franca*. It provided the basis for Behasa Indonesia, the language created after the Second World War, which also contains many Dutch words, sometimes changed beyond recognition. Because the local people could not pronounce an 'f' or 'v', these were substituted by 'p'. A good example is the word 'envelope' that became *amplop*.

The spelling of many Malay words changed in Behasa Indonesia: 'oe' became 'u', 'dj' became 'j' and 'tj' became 'c', 'j' became 'y'. The result is that Poeloe is now Pulu, Djogjakarta is Jogyakarta and Atjeh is Aceh, for example.

The daily language of the internment camps contained many Malay (Indonesian) words and sometimes Japanese words. The common language between the internees and the guards was Malay, since many local men had taken jobs as *soekarillas*, volunteer local soldiers. In some camps one of the women spoke Japanese and could act as interpreter.

The diary and letters at the core of this book were written in Dutch. In translating them, I have tried to use colloquial English to stay true to the spirit of the originals. The poetry that was contained in many of the letters is a different matter. Here I admit defeat and salute anyone who can translate rhymes and meter into even passable English. For that reason the poetry has mostly been described. The original text in Dutch appears in Appendix B.

Here and there in the text money is mentioned. The Japanese introduced the yen for their dealings with the internees, but among themselves and with the locals outside the fence, the internees bartered in pre-war Dutch money, the guilder, which is abbreviated to fl. (for florin, an earlier name of the currency). The pre-war exchange rate was approximately US$1 = fl. 2.50. Those days were long ago, so it is useful to remember that $100 in 1940 would be equivalent to $1,434 today.

Superscribed numbers in the text refer to sources of pictures and text, listed in the bibliography.

## A VOICE FROM THE PAST

"DAD, WHAT'S WITH this box?" In my hands I held a plain wooden box, about the size of a shoebox, that I had just found in the tool shed of my parents' home in Holland. Clearly it was quite old. What intrigued me was that it had our family name stencilled on the bottom.

My father looked at it with surprise. "Where did you find that? I had no idea we still had that." He told me he'd had a *tukan kaju*, a carpenter in Sumatra, make two boxes, this one and its double, when he'd heard that the Japanese were coming. "One for your mother and one for me. They have false bottoms. During the three-and-a-half years we were in the concentration camps, the Japs never discovered our secret."

"Can I have it?" I collected boxes, although usually they were a bit smaller than this, and this one fascinated me. My father nodded, his attention already on his paper again. He did not seem to want to handle the box or look at it more closely.

I found the second box, as well as the keys, and took them home after my visit.

One night, some months later, my eye fell on one of the boxes and I thought idly: I wonder what that false bottom looks like? I carried it over to the table and took a good look at it: the wood was plain and very dark brown, almost black. The top had a metal handle, now rusted, that lay flat on the wood. Its corners had worn two faint half moons on either side. On the left of the handle were some deep gashes in the wood. It looked as if someone had tried to push it into too narrow a hiding place. Had they been in a hurry to hide the box from the Japanese during one of the sudden house searches during their years of internment? The top slid open smoothly in its carved tracks. On one side a lock had been fitted. I took the key from inside the box and tried the lock. It wouldn't budge.

I turned the box over and saw the text that had originally drawn my attention. On the lighter-coloured bottom, the word JONGBLOED was stencilled in bold black letters four centimetres in height. In spite of heavy scratches, the letters were still clear. The bottom was fixed with screws placed midway along the four sides with two on each side of the well-worn corners. One screw was missing; the others lay flush with the surface of the wood. They turned easily when I took a screwdriver to them, as if they had only recently been tightened.

As I lifted off the sturdy bottom, I saw a space about ten millimetres deep, filled with tightly folded pieces of paper. Carefully I took out one of the small parcels. I recognized the minute handwriting as my father's. 'For bébé Marijcke', it read. I felt a shiver run down my spine. A letter from my father to me? The second scrap I looked at bore the text: 'When the pains of the delivery have gone, you may feel like a letter from your loving husband.'

In all there were twelve letters, dating from two weeks before my birth in 1943 until about six months after. Incredibly, those scraps of paper had stayed there all this time, hidden from view, and safe from damage. Not even woodworms had attacked the ancient paper. Slowly I turned the box in my hands with an increasing sense of amazement.

The partition between the box and the secret compartment was made of a very thin sheet of glossy, light brown wood. I sniffed at it, thinking it might be sandalwood, but if it was, the sweet smell was very faint and I couldn't be sure. It was impossible to see how that nameless Indonesian craftsman had fit the sheet of wood into the walls of the box. If I had not known about the double bottom, I would never have guessed it was anything but a simple box. The secret space was not large but it would be enough for a few documents, paper money and bits of jewellery. I wondered what would have been kept in the accessible part of the box: some tools (the screwdriver), needles and thread, pencils and buttons, bits of string and rubber bands maybe?

The other box, my father's, was empty. If I had opened that one first, I might never have found the letters.

I marveled at the fact that the box and its fragile contents had survived fifty-two years and a dozen moves across three continents. Carefully I unfolded the delicate bits of paper. It was clear that these were very personal letters. I wanted to read them but felt I had to ask my parents' permission first. I called and told my father what I had found. "Really?" he said. "That's amazing. Of course you can read them." Neither he nor my mother ever asked to see the letters, then or later. For them, some things were apparently better left in the past.

It was dawn when I finished reading, exhausted by emotion.

I had always been aware of my parents' years in the Japanese concentration camps, although they rarely talked about their experiences. What I knew about it came mainly from a handwritten diary that my mother gave me long ago. The diary had survived all our moves intact, apart from some damage to the cover. That cover was of pale blue card with the picture of a cherubic baby on the front. The pages, now yellowing, were covered with my mother's spidery handwriting, in pencil. In between the pages were drawings of me in various stages of babyhood, the hand-made birth announcement, and a folded piece of paper with a curl of soft blond hair.

I cannot remember when my mother gave it to me. I always knew it was there, that it was something special, something for and about me. It was a record and held a lot of information, but my mother's emotions and thoughts about the camp situations come only rarely through in the diary text. On the other hand, the letters that I had just read were so personal, so direct. They transported me back into those terrible war years and reflected the emotions of a young man who had just become a father but did not, at the time he was writing, know for certain if he would ever see his daughter. I was two years old when that day finally arrived.

ALTHOUGH FOR MANY YEARS I have wanted to tell the story of those war years, I did not set about doing it until after I retired in 2003. Over the next two or three years I typed out the handwritten texts. When I started I only wanted to make the text accessible for my brother and his children.

Both sets of documents were written in tiny script, with the sentences all strung together without breaks. This was to save paper, which was a scarce commodity in the camps. The letters I found were written in pencil on small pieces of very thin paper: cigarette paper? They cover the period from mid-August 1943 to April 1944. There were no letters from my mother, although clearly she had written many.

My father's handwriting was always excellent and that is what helped when I came to decipher it. Still, it was so difficult that I had to leave the job at times.

But I always turned back to it, for it felt as if I was doing something worthwhile.

Somewhere along the line came the idea that other people than just my family would be interested in the story. I decided to put together a book in English, and so I started to translate the text. It was only when I was doing this that the full impact of the events of those war years hit me. Having to find the right words for my mother's difficult circumstances and my father's intense longing brought it all to life.

My father's letters were folded into small packets of nine centimetres by three centimetres, fastened by a tiny strip of sticking plaster. This made sense in the light of what he had told me long before I discovered them, that he and my mother communicated by means of letters that were smuggled between camps in the hollowed-out heel of a *teklek*, the wooden sandal, worn by one of the employees of his company.

My father had also said that the man would have been beaten up or even killed if his role in the communication had been discovered. Presumably that danger was one of the reasons why the letters stopped when they did.

I remembered my father's story about this man when I was in Medan in 1974 and decided to look him up. He was not easy to find but I had help from the then-director of the company my father used to work for, where the man had been employed until he retired. Although he was only in his sixties, he seemed ancient, as he sat on a bamboo *bale-bale* in front of his small house in a back street of Medan, enveloped in a pungent clove-cloud of *kretek* cigarette smoke.

"*Apa kabar, pak*," I greeted him as I approached.

"*Kabar baik*," came the standard reply.

In my halting Indonesian, I introduced myself as the daughter of *Tuan* Jongbloed, who sent his greetings. He showed no surprise or pleasure. In fact, he seemed a bit timid. It was a reaction that I had come across before when I worked in Indonesia during the early 1970s. '*Malu*' is the word that describes it, a mixture of shyness and embarrassment that occurs when the person does not quite understand what you are talking about but does not want to be so impolite as to show his lack of understanding.

I wanted to ask him about his role in conveying the news of my birth to my father in prison, but my Indonesian (more geared to medical terms) was not up to more than:

"*Saja lahir waktu perang* – I was born in the war, do you remember?"

He nodded slowly, but I had no idea whether he had understood who I was.

I wanted to ask him how real the danger had been of getting caught and how he had travelled – by foot or bicycle? Had he had accomplices among the guards of the prison? And how had he managed to get the notes to my mother in the camp? Had he thrown them across the fence or given them to someone trustworthy? At that time I did not know yet that I would get to hold those letters in my hand one day. I wanted to ask him if he had been afraid – but even if my Indonesian had been subtle enough to ask this politely, I doubt that I would have had an answer.

Thirty years later, as I worked my way slowly through the documents, at times I ran into passages that I could not understand because of abbreviations and references to previous events. By then I could no longer ask my parents who had died shortly after one another in the late 1990s. I could have kicked myself for not having started this task while they were still alive.

Fortunately my parents' library and my own both held many books about the war in Indonesia, most as yet unread by me. The standard work about the Japanese civilian camps by Dr D van Velden provided reliable factual information. I found more direct personal accounts in published diaries, one of which ran practically parallel with my mother's diary.

My father's library held one volume of the extensive collection of diaries called *Noord Sumatra in Oorlogstijd* (North Sumatra during the war) that had been compiled between 1991 and 1995 by ex-internees. I mentioned this book to a friend. "Oh," she told me, "I have the whole collection." I borrowed it for a year and worked my way through most of the fourteen volumes. In them I found diaries that covered the second camp my father had been in and about which I didn't have much information except a few stories he had told me. These diaries provided me with an enormous amount of detail that fitted well with what my parents had written and said.

My research on the Internet inevitably led me to other books, some of which I added to my library. Often they were about other camps but comparing the situations gave me a better understanding of what conditions had been like for my parents.

One book that was particularly helpful in this way was the account by Ann Jacobs about the camp years which she wrote as a novel in 1947. *Ontwortelden* was even more interesting than the diaries because in the safety of being free she had no worries about discovery and therefore could write about her fear and hatred of the Japanese without risking repercussions while at the same time recording inconsequential things such as observations of nature or funny incidents. Her account of the terrible journey of the women and children from Medan to Rantau Prapat in 1945 made me feel as if I was part of it, or rather part of it again: I have no recollection of being there.

One accidental contact that meant a lot to me was the result of a curious incident that happened in the early 1980s when my brother was a pilot with KLM. On one trip from Lanzarote, he was flying the plane on which my parents were returning from vacation. My father had been given the privilege of witnessing the take-off from a seat in the cockpit.

The captain, who was not piloting the plane that day, turned to my brother after my father had returned to the cabin and said: "Is your father's first name Henk?" When my brother confirmed this, the captain immediately left his seat and went to see my father. It turned out that they had known each other during the last year of internment in Si Rengo Rengo camp. When my brother told me this, I phoned his colleague who in turn shared his memories, many of them painful. Most of his information is included in the chapter on Si Rengo Rengo.

THIS YEAR IT is sixty-five years since the end of the war in the Pacific. It's a lifetime ago. The anniversary will be a time of remembering – with joy about the end of the misery and suffering of so many millions of people, and with regret and sadness about the enormous loss of life that accompanied the final acts of war.

In the years of researching background information for this book, I have learned much that I didn't know, digging into archives and speaking with survivors of those dark times. Their recollections and the diaries of fellow prisoners have gone a long way to corroborating what my parents told me.

What I also discovered was a sense of profound personal gratitude. As I sit typing this, sipping a coffee, nibbling on a biscuit, I am acutely aware that I barely know what a hunger pang is. This morning when I took care of the horses I had boots on for trudging through the mud. I have no other life depending on me (if you don't count the animals). The fact that I sit here in a comfortable house in a wonderful place I owe to a thirty-six year old woman who shared her meagre portions of food with me and courted death to save my life.

This is a story of two brave and loving people, Hendrik Jongbloed and Maria Catharina Antoinette Ochel – Henk and Rie. It is also the story of my birth and first years. It is a story of survival.

## CHAPTER I

# EQUALS AND OPPOSITES

HENK AND RIE made an attractive couple, a marriage of equals and opposites. He was confident, the archetypal solid citizen, an accountant by training, a businessman who could be relied on to run substantial overseas enterprises with efficiency and dedication. She was an artist, a singer and concert pianist who needed the applause of an audience or the approval of a loved one. They risked the wrath of the church and the establishment in an altogether stricter moral climate to be together. That they were willing to do so speaks volumes of their strength of character, something they would need in abundance.

The years of their youth were turbulent. Rie was born in 1907 and Henk in 1913, so they were children during the First World War, teenagers during the Roaring Twenties, and starting their adult life during the Great Depression. Another world war would disrupt their early life together but no one was aware of that when they started courting.

When she was in her late teens, Rie studied at the Amsterdam conservatory. She met a fellow musician and married him when she was nineteen. Most likely this was an act of desperation on her part. She was lonely, for her parents were divorced and she had lost contact with her mother. Her father was a sailor in the navy and rarely ashore. In her teens she was taken care of by her cousin Nel, who was ten years older and who – Rie used to say – was her only relative.

Her husband was an organist and may have been a teacher at the conservatory. He gave music lessons in their home. Some years later, Henk became one of his pupils and met his teacher's wife before and after the lessons. They fell in love and in 1934 Rie left her husband and her six-year-old son for Henk. The guilt feelings that she carried with her for abandoning her son Frits may have contributed to her need for the support of religion. In later years, she would be reunited with that son, but that was a long way in the future.

Even without this problem, times were hard enough for young people. Unemployment was spreading throughout Europe in the early 1930s, crippling industry and commerce, undermining traditional social structures and creating fertile conditions for unrest. In Holland, shipping and trading – mainstays of the economy – were particularly badly affected. The prospects for a newly qualified accountant, no matter how diligent or capable, were not promising.

In order to escape the hardships of the depression, Henk decided around 1935 to find work in the Dutch East Indies. This decision may have had more to do with the fact that both his father and one of his elder brothers, Karel, had been there than with job opportunities, because at that time the Indies were also suffering from the global downturn in the economy. Demand for raw materials such as rubber, and the luxury items coffee and tea – the mainstays of the colony's export trade – had dropped considerably and consequently the production of these cultures decreased to a quarter of what it was in the heydays at the beginning of the century. Still, Henk found a job with the Colonial Bank in Soerabaja in East Java, where he specialised in the administration of sugar plantations and sugar mills.

The plan was for Rie to follow after a while, when Henk had settled in his new job and all the necessary formalities for their wedding had been completed. In the meantime, she rented a small room from a landlady and had a difficult time trying to make a living as a classical singer and pianist. She played the piano for the silent movies and sang recitals for the radio.

Later Rie recalled: "I was always short of money. I often had no money for food, but I would always make sure I had a bunch of flowers in my room.

"I remember that when I had received my very first payment for a recital, I went home by tram. When I got off the tram, I threw away what I thought was my tram ticket, only to find out when I got home that I had thrown away my entire pay!"

She also somehow spent money on jewellery. Her favourite necklace was a long string of cut milk-glass beads, long enough to be knotted and still reach to the waist – a real Roaring Twenties relic. I still have them and wear them often.

During these years, Rie often went to Nel's home for lunch. Nel's daughter Els recently recalled that she sometimes brought her son, little Frits: "A beautiful shy little boy with blond curls. I never understood why she did not take him with her when she went East." Rie never mentioned Frits until the 1950s. She never explained why she had abandoned him. Maybe she was forced to do so by the terms of her divorce.

When Henk left for the Indies, his mother invited Rie to stay with her. She had noticed that her future daughter-in-law was getting very thin and that may have helped her decide to take her in. This was quite a step for the old lady, as she was not very happy with the prospect of having an excommunicated, divorced older woman as the wife of her beloved youngest son, but if it had to be, then at least the girl should be healthy!

*Oma* Jongbloed lived in an apartment above a milk shop on the corner of a small square in Amsterdam. She was not in fact very old – just fifty-seven at the time – but she just seemed that way. She had a huge goitre and bulging eyes, and she was painfully thin. She was a very determined, strict and ambitious

*Opa and Oma Jongbloed, seated at left, at son Karel's wedding, early 1930s. Piet has his pipe in his mouth; Henk is holding his.*

lady, dictating the lives of her children and her husband who became an alcoholic later in life. *Opa* by all accounts was a mild and humorous man, who originally was a pastry chef. In the early years of the century he sailed as a cook on a ship to Indonesia. Later he became a salesman of bakery goods – a job that gave him the opportunity to frequent bars and cafés.

MY FATHER WAS the youngest of five, nine years younger than his oldest sister, Annie. Although he got on well with all of his siblings, he always spoke of Annie, who was a creative free-thinker (the only one who did not stay within the Reformed church), with special admiration and affection. Perhaps that was partly because she was also the only one of the family who did not survive the war. Annie was also instrumental in the direction Henk's life would take. As a young boy, my father was fascinated by airplanes and the newly developing aviation industry. He was determined to become a pilot. Then one day, he entered a room where Annie was practising juggling cones. One cone hit him forcibly in his eye, effectively blinding it. That was the end of his dream of flying.*

His oldest brother, Piet, was a bit of a tear-away when he was young. Following his mother's wishes, he studied theology and became a minister, but when I knew him later in life, he never quite seemed to fit that profession. For a start, he owned a Bordeaux-red Yamaha motor bike. When he came to visit us, he would roar onto the school playground, spouting gravel as he swerved to a standstill. I think my brother and I then rode back with him to our house, but I don't remember that. I only remember his noisy arrival, which both excited and embarrassed me. My brother, who was named Peter after *Oom* Piet, remembers being pillion passenger on that bike as they rode home cross-country – straight through the forest – to the great envy of his schoolmates.

Another stunt that the two Petes loved performing was to cross the canal without using the bridge. They would stand on the quay of the canal in front of *oom* Piet's house as the drawbridge went up to let a barge through. The large ones were almost as wide as the canal. They would step from the quay on to the deck of the passing boat, walk across and step off again on the other side, to the encouraging shouts of the onlookers. You wouldn't get away with that now, but they did.

*Oom* Piet had a fondness for fish that I shared. Muiden, the small town where he was the minister, is situated on the shore of the IJsselmeer and on market days, fish stalls line the streets and squares. No one in our family liked fish the way *oom* Piet and I did. His wife, *tante* Miep, couldn't stand the smell of fish in her house, so my uncle and I would sneak out to the stall where the fish that had been caught that morning was fried. *Lekkerbekjes*, they were

---

* Henk's fascination with anything airborne remained and was transferred to the next generations. His son became a pilot and Henk vicariously enjoyed his career as if it had been his own. When his grandson followed suit in 2010, it was just as he had always predicted.

*Henk and his siblings Puck, Annie, Karel and Piet, about 1925.*

called, mouthfuls of delight! This was battered whiting, deepfried. Or *kibbeling*, deepfried cod filets in spicy batter. The best treat of all was sole, fried in butter. I sucked the soft white flesh off the bone and saved the crispy fins and tail for last. We ate them from a piece of paper, with our hands dripping with butter. Cholesterol? We hadn't even heard of it!

Unlike Piet, my father's other brother, Karel, was buttoned down and something of an oddity in the family. Like Henk, he was an accountant; like Henk, he also went to the Indies for a while, but he came back to marry the extremely restrained daughter of a theology professor. Although he did have the well-known Jongbloed sense of humour, he seemed to me to be rather distant and cold. My parents used to say he was different before he married.

My father's youngest sister, Puck, was a grade-school teacher. She was a warm-hearted, cheerful person, who liked children. She never had any of her own and only married (her widowed high school sweetheart) when she was in her forties. I have a memory of her from a furlough in 1950 when we stayed at my grandmother's apartment. I would cuddle up with my aunt in the mornings and she would tell me a story. I lay watching her face where a small blob of spittle in the corner of her mouth would stretch and collapse, stretch and collapse, again and again, as she spoke. I don't remember the stories.

FOR MY MOTHER, this was a pleasant period – finally she had a family: Henk's siblings and their friends, who welcomed her into their lives. They included the newcomer in the picnics and games on the beach, cycling weekends in the flat polders and sailing trips on the Loosdrecht lakes, where they rented a wooden cottage that could only be reached by rowboat. They sent pictures of these happy times to young Henk in the far-off Indies. He must have enjoyed seeing that his wife-to-be was embraced so warmly by his family and friends.

That affection was evident when, many years later, I would visit *tante* Miep regularly. She shared an apartment with her two elderly sisters ("Together we are 239 years old," they would giggle). They had known my mother before she went to the East. They loved to tell me, over tea and cookies, about that time. They had all lived in the same neighbourhood, the Watergraafsmeer, quite far from the centre of Amsterdam and they used to walk to work together. "But your mother walked so slowly. We always said she walked like a queen – with slow, measured steps."

Rie was shy by nature and had very little self-confidence. Being almost six years older than my father, she was always afraid that she would lose him to a younger woman. She needed a lot of reassurance and would often ask him, as well as us children in later years: "Do you love me?" or "Did I do well?" The artist in her needed applause.

On stage she was a different person. She had a pleasant alto voice and sang solo concerts, recitals of the songs of Wolff and Schubert, as well as the alto parts of the Bach passions and other sacred music. Of all her broad repertoire, I loved the spirituals most. Somehow the emotions of joy and sadness that are contained in those old folk songs struck a chord with her and she sang them with passion: '*Little David, play on your harp, hallelu, hallelu!*'

She looked like a queen in her evening dress and jewellery, with her regal bearing – a classical beauty. I remember watching her while she got ready for a concert. I'd be seated on the bed, dangling my feet, while she was in front of her mirror, inserting long pearl pendants in her pierced ears and slipping diamond and emerald rings onto her beautifully manicured fingers. She applied her lipstick with care, catching first her lower lip with the upper and then the other way around to smooth the gloss evenly. We did not talk much: it would have broken the spell. She was already concentrating on her performance, and I felt her hidden excitement and tension. The finishing touch came when she dabbed her cheeks with rouge and powdered her face. I still have her silver powder box, but the powder is long gone and its scent remains only in my memory.

Gardening was her other great passion; it played an important part in her life. She loved to make things grow and had great success both with gardens and with indoor plants. It was in her garden that she found peace of mind. It was a place where she was simply happy without the constant need to perform and please.

I remember times during which life was on an even keel and the bogeymen of the past were temporarily in hiding, when my mother was lots of fun to be with, and she could let go and act like a giggly teenager. The two of us had wonderful forays into the big city of Amsterdam where we used to go for our piano lessons.

She was usually rather docile but from time to time she'd get set on an idea and then she'd follow it through – like when she decided she wanted to learn to drive. We were living in Indonesia at the time. My father was not keen, but she persuaded our chauffeur to teach her. During a lesson, she missed a turn on a rather busy shopping street. She careened into an open shop, having scooped up a local lady on a bicycle, fortunately at a very slow speed so no one was hurt. That put an end to that effort, but not to her determination. A few years later, when we were living in Holland and while my father was on a six-month tour of duty in Indonesia, she took driving lessons and passed her exam. When my father returned, we went to pick him up at the airport.

He was surprised to see us alone. "Who brought you?" he asked.

"I drove," she said, pride and defiance radiating from her face, "and I'm driving back, too!"

This show of defiance was rare. Normally she was happy enough playing the submissive wife. Henk did not think she could look after herself. He was so much better organised. I think, however, that it was an act on her part. She quite liked being spoiled and cosseted.

Henk had a completely different temperament. He was immensely self-assured and if that trait had not been combined with an equally strong sense of justice and humanity, he would have been intolerable. To many people he seemed arrogant and hard, but those who got to know him better would glimpse a heart full of compassion. He was very considerate of other people's feelings. When in the 1960s he was the director of a light bulb factory, he employed people with mental or physical handicaps. He reasoned that rather than donating money to help the handicapped, jobs would allow them to earn their own money and with that he gave them pride. His fellow citizens put his name forward for a medal and in 1974 he received a knighthood in the Order of Orange Nassau in recognition of his special type of social work.

His most important quality, however, was his zany sense of humour. It most often appeared in moments of duress. Whenever we found ourselves in a rather unpleasant situation (slow and bad service in a restaurant, terrible weather during a camping trip, a flea infestation in our house) he would start making remarks about the situation that soon had us all in stitches.

He was extremely neat and organised, so the more Bohemian attitude of my mother and me used to drive him nuts. He always looked impeccable, never a spot on his shirt or tie. He used pearl tiepins to keep the tie tacked to his shirt, later to be displaced by a special pin that my brother had given him. It was the pin that my brother had been awarded in recognition of 10,000 hours of flying with KLM, and that became his special favourite, reflecting his pride in his son's achievement. He attached the pin to the shirt in such a way that the tie made a neat little bulge below the knot, a kind of 'Henk trademark'.

As an accountant, he managed other people's finances meticulously, but he never taught us how to handle our finances. I never quite understood why he stood by and watched me get into financial trouble which could have easily been avoided. Maybe he believed in learning by your mistakes. Both my parents were extremely generous and gave away lots of money to all sorts of causes and charities. "There'll be less left for you," he used to say, and I would assure him that I could take care of myself.

In contrast to my mother, he did not suffer from a moody temperament. He was always the same: moderately optimistic, stable and unflappable. His name should have been Petrus, the rock.

## 2

# EASTWARD

IN THE DUTCH East Indies, where the young couple planned to set up home, colonial relationships were undergoing great change. The seventeenth and eighteenth century exploitation of the local people had given way to the enlightened approach of the *Binnenlands Bestuur* (BB, the civil service) which was dedicated to involving locals in governing the provinces and to developing the infrastructure of roads, railways, schools and ports. Unfortunately it was too little, too late. Many wanted to be free of the Dutch colonial yoke and unrest was brewing everywhere. The colony was on its last legs.

Henk disembarked in 1936 into a country that was still an integral part of the Dutch kingdom. Dutch interests had dominated this vast archipelago of 17,000 islands almost uninterrupted since the beginning of the seventeenth century. But the spice trade – the prize for which successive European powers had fought – had long since given way, in terms of commercial importance, to vast plantations of rubber, tea and coffee and industrial installations exploiting 'black gold', oil. This meant that the 1930s colonial was more likely to be an accountant or estate manager than the soldier-trader of earlier, more repressive eras. Unfortunately the legacy of those times, when the methods used to conquer new areas and subjugate the local tribes were brutal, lived on in the local population's general hatred of Europeans, however benign their behaviour. Eventually this led to the founding of independence movements and native political parties including, in the Dutch East Indies, the Indonesian National Party whose leaders would declare independence in 1945.

Many of the early Dutch who had settled in the archipelago, it is true, behaved like lords and masters, exploited the local labourers to increase the profits of their companies and in general did little to provide the local population with schooling, health care and social security. Of course, during the nineteenth century this was happening in colonial outposts everywhere.

The situation in the Dutch East Indies in those days was described in detail in a book published in 1860 that became famous for pricking the collective conscience of the Dutch. *Max Havelaar* was a thinly disguised attack on colonialism that drew the attention of the Dutch to the fact that the wealth they enjoyed caused immense suffering in the colonies, something they had been unaware of until then. The author, Eduard Douwes Dekker, a clerk and later assistant-resident, published the book under the pen name Multatuli, which means 'I suffered a lot'. In the novel the protagonist, Max Havelaar, tried to battle against the corrupt government system in the Indies. In this system the indigenous populations of the islands were forced to grow 'cultures', commercially valuable crops of tobacco, tea and coffee, instead of staple foods such as rice. They were harassed by tax collectors who were paid by commission which caused widespread abuse of power. In addition, local rulers called 'regents' had to be supported in the lavish lifestyle that befitted an oriental person of power by the people they ruled. The double taxation resulted in the poverty and starvation of local farmers and their families.

Multatuli's book played a key role in shaping and modifying Dutch colonial policy in the nineteenth and early twentieth century. It also caused controversy because the Dutch did not like the way their compatriots were depicted and

*A period photo of the Colonial Bank in Soerabaja, Henk's first employer in the Indies. Photo courtesy of Tropenmuseum.*

the Indonesians were unhappy about the way in which they were described, either as cruel rulers or as humble, unresisting slaves.

ABOUT A YEAR after Henk had arrived in the Indies, Rie received the news that she could join him. However, there was a problem: unmarried women were not given an entry permit to the colony, and without a permit she could not attend her own wedding. Fortunately there was a way around this: to get married 'with the glove', as it was popularly called. It was a legal procedure, officially termed 'marrying by power of attorney'. The groom in the Dutch East Indies applied to the Dutch courts for a marriage permit. When this was granted, a friend of the family stood in for the groom in a civil ceremony, wearing white gloves. The gloves were later handed to the groom. The women who were married in this way were known as 'little gloves'.

*Left: Henk was in a sugar cane field on Java on 30 October 1937, the day of his civil marriage in Amsterdam. Right: Rie sailing to the Indies.*

On the day of this first 'wedding' in October 1937, Henk was walking through a sugar cane field on Java with his boss. Looking at his watch, he said: "Do you know what's happening this very moment? I'm getting married!" It was never mentioned but it is likely a nice bottle of champagne was popped that evening. Back in Amsterdam, the festivities within the strictly Christian Reformed Jongbloed family would not have included any alcoholic beverages. Henk's father, however, may have celebrated with his favourite tipple in the pub.

Rie's journey by ship to the Indies was a long one. Although her passage had been fully paid, she had not realised that you needed money to pay for drinks and to tip the crew. On the fifth day out, she had only one coin of fl. 2.50 left. That evening, she decided to throw caution to the wind and

*The bridal pair after their wedding in Soerabaja, Rie happy, Henk solemn, and holding the white gloves used in the civil ceremony back in Holland.*

*The newlyweds on honeymoon in the mountains.*

wagered her entire 'fortune' in a tortoise race. Luck was on her side: she won the pot, which enabled her to sail on without money worries.

In December 1937, Henk and Rie were married in church (had she been forgiven, or did her new husband's piety absolve her?) in Soerabaja on the island of Java. The wedding took place only a few days after Rie had arrived in the tropics. It was not without incident. At exactly the moment when the pastor asked her the important question, a number of *larongs*, flying termites, dived into and under her veil. She later recalled: "I had no idea what they were and whether they would bite. My answer came out very squeaky but I don't think pappie even noticed." The picture of the bridal pair shows Rie happy, veil intact, and Henk looking very young and solemn, amidst masses of flowers.

The couple spent four wonderfully romantic years in East Java. Henk immersed himself in the administrative side of running plantations and Rie was able to spend a lot of time on her music, giving piano and singing lessons and singing in concerts. Sometimes, she recalled many years later, she accompanied Henk on trips to the plantations and revelled in Java's natural beauty. It must have felt to them that they were living in another world; in many ways, they were. At that time, Soerabaja was a busy port, trading centre and naval base, the largest city in the district with a good sized expatriate population. The leafy suburbs where they lived consisted of roomy and comfortable stone bungalows with large folding doors and windows for ventilation and overhanging roofs to protect against the regular heavy rains. The tropical heat and humidity meant it was a constant battle to maintain houses and grounds and each household employed several servants for that task.

It was a pleasant life for Henk and Rie, with the mountains and the sea close by for trips on weekends and vacations. Old family photo albums show them

*Left: Henk and Rie shared a house with friends in Soerabaja. Right: Moving into her new home.*

on mountaintops after arduous climbs, in hot water springs, at the bull races in Madura and riding horseback – "uncomplicated happy days", as Henk referred to them later in letters. The events that convulsed Europe from September 1939 were far away but the impact of war began to be felt. By the time they were due to sail back to Holland for home leave, it was no longer possible.

Their one regret during these happy days was that Rie did not become pregnant. There was little chance of this, because during her first marriage she had had an operation in which one ovary was removed completely and of the other, only a quarter was left. The gynaecologist who performed this operation told her that it was very unlikely she would ever have children again.

In 1941, Henk and Rie moved to the city of Medan on Sumatra, where Henk had taken a job as the secretary of the Belgian company Sipef* that owned rubber, tea, coffee and palm oil plantations. Leaving Java was a wrench for Rie. She had felt at home there. As for Henk, he had to jump in at the deep end because the director, Klaas ten Velde, had just been called up into the Dutch Indies army (KNIL) to train for the expected invasion of the Japanese and there was no time to show the newcomer the ropes.

Henk worked in a large white office building, set in a park-like garden in the centre of town. His work meant he often had to travel to the fifteen plantations that he administered to check the books and pay the workers.

These journeys of Henk's to outlying holdings sometimes took him to the northern district of Atjeh (now Aceh) which had a long history of political independence and fierce resistance to control by outsiders. It is no coincidence that in the war to come, the Atjeh guerrilla fighters initially welcomed the Japanese invasion as a means of overthrowing the hated colonial power.

For centuries, the Sultanate of Atjeh had been the most wealthy, powerful

---

* Société Internationale de Plantations et de Finance (Sipef) was set up in 1919 in Brussels to promote and manage plantation companies in tropical and sub-tropical areas. Today Sipef's operations are worldwide.

*Sipef offices, Medan, circa 1941.*

and cultivated state in the Malacca Straits region. Part of its influence was due to its strategic location for controlling regional trade. In addition, in the early nineteenth century, it produced more than half the world's supply of black pepper. The pepper trade brought wealth to the sultanate.

Tensions with the Dutch hit breaking point in the late nineteenth century when Atjeh was apparently considering talks aimed at giving the US access to the region. The Dutch colonial government declared war on Atjeh in 1873 and sent several expeditions into the region, with minimal success. Even after the sultan's palace had been captured, guerrilla warfare continued for another decade as Atjeh remained stubbornly independent.

That changed after 1898 when Major J B Van Heutsz was proclaimed governor of Atjeh. He found cooperative *uleebelang*, hereditary chiefs, who would support the Dutch in the countryside. Any remaining resistance was dealt with harshly; villages were destroyed, their inhabitants killed. By 1904, most of Atjeh was under Dutch control, and had an indigenous government which cooperated with the colonial state. The cost of subjugation in human life was estimated at 50,000 to 100,000 dead, and over a million wounded. Even so, colonial influence in the remote highland areas of Atjeh was never substantial, and limited guerrilla resistance remained.

When the Japanese attacked Sumatra in 1942, the Atjeh guerrillas saw this as an opportunity to gain the longed-for independence. However, this never materialised and Atjeh, with its substantial natural resources, including oil and gas (the gas reserves being among the largest in the world), continued striving throughout the second half of the twentieth century for self-rule and independence from Indonesia. A peace agreement was finally signed with the Indonesian government on 15 August 2005, in the aftermath of the 2004 tsunami disaster.

Sixty-five years earlier, as Henk and Rie established themselves in Medan, it was man-made disaster that loomed on the horizon.

## 3

# WORLD AT WAR

It is difficult to imagine what was going on in the minds of Henk and Rie in the Far East as, in the meantime, the rest of the world was fast falling into chaos. War had broken out in Europe and contact with the family back home became difficult.

One card still reached them, written on 10 May 1940 by Henk's eldest brother, Piet, who was then a chaplain in the Dutch army. This was the day on which Germany invaded Holland. He wrote:

> ...Now hell has broken out in our country.... This morning at 3.30am I woke up to the thunder of the anti-aircraft guns... I am very worried, especially about Mom. She was supposed to go into hospital tomorrow in Amsterdam. Will that still happen? Will she be evacuated? And will she, with her weak heart, be able to cope with that? We don't know, just as we don't know what the future of Holland will be... I can't say much about how the fighting is going, everything is quite chaotic. The mood of the soldiers is grim and serious. What they'll be able to save, God only knows, but at least their honour... Will there be any contact between us? And

what will the fate of Indië* be? Will Japan attack and will you also get into trouble? May God prevent that!'

This was to be the last news from Holland until November 1945.

Closer to home, on the Asian front, the Japanese were waging a war that they euphemistically called 'the establishment of the Greater East Asia Co-Prosperity Sphere'. It had already started in China in the late thirties and continued in September 1940 with the occupation of the port city of Haiphong in present-day Vietnam, then part of French Indo-China which also comprised Cambodia and Laos. Japan then allied itself with Germany and Italy. Initially the plan was to infiltrate South East Asia gradually, not risking a war with England and America.

In July 1941, more Japanese troops were sent to French Indo-China, which caused the USA, followed by England and the Netherlands, to freeze all Japanese assets in their countries. Rather than diminishing the Japanese aspirations to reign over the countries of Greater East Asia, it fanned the flames. Japan's military leaders decided that if war had to be, it had to be soon, as Japan only had oil reserves for two years. The huge oil fields in the Dutch East Indies and Borneo were an obvious target. To ensure safe transport lines between these oil fields and Japan, the Japanese had to move quickly to conquer Singapore, the Philippines, Guam and Wake.

The extent of the front that the Japanese opened was astounding. From Hawaii through the Pacific and South East Asia as far west as the Indian islands, the attacks were carried out almost simultaneously. They even made brief forays on the East African and West American coasts and Australia, but these attempts were not followed through.

The attack on Pearl Harbor on 7 December 1941 eliminated most of the

---

* Indië, often 'our Indië' or the Dutch East Indies, is what the Dutch called the colony, to distinguish it from India (British India) and the West Indies.

*Piet, the army chaplain.*

American Pacific fleet and immediately brought declarations of war from the USA and Britain, with the Netherlands joining in as their ally. A few hours earlier, the Japanese had invaded northern Malacca and south-east Thailand and attacked Western concessions in Shanghai. Soon after the attack on Pearl Harbor, Singapore was bombed and the first Japanese landed on Batan island in the north of the Philippines, followed by the first air attacks on Guam, Hong Kong and Wake. The same day, Japanese Emperor Hirohito declared war on the United States and Great Britain. War against the Netherlands was not declared until 12 January 1942, although by that time the Japanese had already occupied the Tambelan islands and bombed several areas in the Dutch East Indies.

With their declarations of war, Britain and Holland confined all Japanese living in their territories – actions which were to have consequences for the foreign civilian populations of South East Asia. The USA did not at first act against the many Japanese who had been living, often for generations, in

American territory – especially Hawaii – but later it too rounded up and confined Japanese civilians to camps.

The Japanese advanced like a tidal wave. On 10 December 1941, the British cruisers HMS *Prince of Wales* and HMS *Repulse* were sunk and the American air force bases in the Philippines were destroyed. Guam was taken. The Japanese landed at several places on the north coast of oil-rich Borneo and reached the refinery and port town of Balikpapan on 24 January. They found that the oil installations had been destroyed by the Europeans, and killed most of them in retaliation. The Dutch troops in Borneo surrendered on 27 March. In Celebes, which later became Sulawesi, the Dutch military, among whom were men from the island of Ambon and Celebes, kept fighting until August, when they were captured by the Japanese. All the Europeans among them were beheaded.

In an attempt to halt the Japanese advance, the American, British, Dutch and Australian (ABDA) forces had united under one command, ABDACOM, in January 1942. However, they were not able to cope with the overwhelming power of the Japanese on all fronts.

The ABDA fleet that was to protect Java was commanded by Vice-Admiral Conrad Helfrich who deployed two strike forces – the Eastern strike force based in Soerabaja under Admiral Karel Doorman and the Western strike force based in the harbour of Batavia. The approaching Japanese were spotted on 25 February and the next day a Royal Navy contingent was sent to the Eastern strike force as reinforcement. The battle that ensued on 27 February in the Java Sea cost the ABDA command six ships, five of which were sunk with large loss of life – including that of Admiral Doorman – and delayed the invasion of Java by just one day.

Singapore had already fallen on 15 February. The same day, Japanese troops landed in southern Sumatra, strategically important because of its huge oil fields. However, here the Territorial Commander of Middle Sumatra had been expecting that attack and mounted an imaginative defensive strategy. General-Major R Th Overakker became famous for what was called the 'circus Overakker'. He and his two thousand mainly untrained men camouflaged trucks to look like tanks and drove them back and forth along the jungle roads, in order to fool the surveying Japanese planes into thinking that there was a large military presence in the middle of Sumatra. This tactic gave the Dutch time to blow up the bridges and the oil refineries: in one act of sabotage, installations worth two billion pre-war dollars were blown to smithereens in Pangkalan Brandan. Overakker's circus also influenced the Japanese army's decision that they needed thirty thousand men to conquer Sumatra, thus reducing the army that was to attack Australia to such an extent that this attack never happened.

The Dutch guerrillas could not hold out long and retreated to the mountains of Atjeh in northern Sumatra. On 28 March, Overakker was captured and taken to Singapore where he was executed in 1945, just before the end of the war. Before he was captured, he gave a written order about Dutch leadership after the war to one of his officers, Klaas ten Velde. In civilian life, this man was Henk's boss at Sipef. Ten Velde gave the document to Henk for safekeeping, and he hid it somewhere in his office.

It was this document that would later get him and many others in trouble with the Japanese.

MANY PEOPLE IN the Dutch East Indies had not believed the Japanese army would attack the colony and considered themselves fortunate as the news from Europe became worse. Henk remained optimistic. "He always said that it was impossible for the Japanese to intern the whole white population of East Indie," Rie wrote many years later. "We consoled ourselves with that thought and lived as if we had years and years of freedom in sight."

From May 1940 onwards, repatriation of women and children to Holland was no longer possible, and in any case, many Dutch were so at home in the colony that they would not consider leaving. The rude awakening came when Medan airfield and the port of Belawan were bombed on 28 December 1941. The Japanese returned on 2 January 1942 for another bombing attack, but after that they left Sumatra alone until March.

Rie remembered the air-raid sirens and the first bombing. She and Henk had been enjoying afternoon tea surrounded by flowers in their garden, the dogs lying quietly at their feet, when they heard the noise of aircraft. "Our dogs became uneasy and fled into the house, the sirens started to yell and small objects dropped from the planes... we heard the awful noise of bombing and we knew it was the beginning of a long time of suffering."

The December bombardment was witnessed by a nun who was a teacher at the St Jozefschool, who wrote: [21]

> One day, while we were taking our siesta, the sirens started wailing and at the same time we heard fast planes pass overhead with machine guns blasting. I tried to get under the bed but it was too low. Soon we heard the planes leaving. What had happened? Judging from the direction in which they had flown they must have targeted the airport. And yes! The first news arrived. Local people had been working on the strip. There was one – just one – plane on the field, a commercial plane. That was the target. They must have expected a field full of fighter planes. Poor old Sumatra did not have a single one! The effect of the machine gunning was terrible. The workers had not been able to escape... seventy people died and many more were wounded.

On Sumatra, which was considered an outlying district, the KNIL consisted of untrained civilians, who were called up just days before the Medan airport attack, and who had no uniforms or weapons.

After southern Sumatra had fallen into Japanese hands, the occupation of northern Sumatra was swift. Japanese troops landed in Atjeh where the local population hailed them as liberators – the tribal people of Atjeh's hatred for the Dutch colonial oppressors was well-known and had often given considerable trouble. Very quickly they learned the folly of trading one oppressor for another.

# ೞೞೞ 4 ೞೞೞ

# THE JAPANESE OCCUPATION

THE DAY STARTED much like any other working day for Henk. Rising early to enjoy the freshness of the morning, he dressed in the 'sharkskin' silk suit that he favoured for its comfort and coolness. He sipped his morning tea, ignoring the fruit salad on the table: he only ate fruit if there was no way to avoid it. Then he rose, kissed his wife goodbye and headed for the office. Rie watched him go and then began her morning routine.

"*Kokkie*, I'd like to have ochra today for dinner, can you get that at the *pasar*?"

"*Saja, mem*," replied her cook. Rie counted out the money and handed it to her. It was a shame she could not go to the market herself, but it was one of those things Dutch *nonjas* just did not do – it would drive the prices up. So she planned her day at home: there were music lessons, and perhaps there would be time for a little gardening. Although it seemed like a normal day, neither Henk nor Rie were particularly relaxed: like everyone else, they listened to the radio and read newspapers. They knew the Japanese were coming.

What they did not know at breakfast on Friday, 13 March 1942, was that by evening Medan would be occupied.

The Japanese soldiers did not march in as victorious conquerors, but arrived in twos and threes on stolen bicycles. Not realising that traffic in the Indies drove on the left, the Japanese pedalled down the wrong side of the road, causing traffic snarls and chaos, to the great amusement of the locals who had gathered to see the invasion. There was no resistance. The few unarmed members of the KNIL who were in the area fled to the mountains where they hoped the dense rain forest would provide cover, but they were taken prisoner within a few days, often because local people betrayed their hiding places. They were paraded around on open trucks and the local population was invited to jeer at them. Few did. Then they were interned in the prisoner of war camp at Gloegoer.

The day of the occupation, leaflets in English were distributed with the following instructions:

The Japanese occupation troops hereby notify that:
1. As of today the banks are closed.
2. As of today the post office is closed.
3. Radio transmission from the Dutch East Indies is forbidden.
4. Any radiographic contact with countries abroad is forbidden.
5. Weapons like rifles and guns have to be handed in to the police.
6. The police of the occupying forces have instructions to keep order as usual and to use weapons if necessary.

From today, March 13th, there is curfew from 9pm till 6 a.m. This means that between those hours no one may leave his residence. Anyone who does not heed this order and is found in the street or outside his house runs the risk of being shot dead without warning.

Medan, March 13th 1942
The Chief of Police

At the last moment before the Japanese invasion, some families from Sumatra moved to Java which many considered impregnable. However, it was conquered in eight days. For many years, the Japanese had had a fifth-column presence in Java and so they knew where the vulnerable spots were. In addition, the Dutch army was under Allied High Command but the promised Allied reinforcements did not arrive. Later, there were bitter recriminations that 'for want of a few ships, a few hundred planes, a few thousand well-armed troops, a country was lost'. This loss would turn out to be not just for the duration of the war. It was also effectively the end of Dutch rule in the East Indies.

Initially, the European families were only confined to their homes, with *atap* fences made from palm leaves restricting contact with the outside world. All houses had to fly the Japanese flag. In the first weeks of occupation, elements among the local population tried to take advantage of the situation by *rampokking* – stealing whatever they could lay their hands on. The Japanese put a stop to this in particularly gruesome ways. Anyone caught red-handed was executed and, as Rie recalled later, "the beheaded bodies of those criminals were left hanging on the trees in the silent streets of Medan." Others had their fingernails pulled out or their hands cut off to deter them from further stealing.

In mid-April, the families in Medan were told to report to collection points spread throughout the city. From there, the men and boys older than sixteen were taken off to one camp. The women were taken to separate camps.

Reminiscing in later years, Rie recalled: "We had just settled into our new house [in Polonia] and the dining room furniture that we had bought was being delivered at the very moment I had to leave with thirty kilos of luggage and a rolled-up mattress – all that was allowed. We were ordered to put all our belongings into one locked room of the house, to prevent things from being stolen." What became of her two white Maltese dogs, groomed for the tropics with 'puppy' cuts, remains a mystery.

Around this time the new Japanese governor of the Northern Province introduced himself via a poster.

I am Lieutenant Yamada...

Since the 8th of December 1941 there is war between Japan on one side, and England America and Holland on the other side. You all know the regulations which the nations of the world have to observe when they are at war.

It has been the great kindness of His Imperial Majesty's Government that in spite of the existing war with the victory for the Japanese, you were allowed hitherto to live in your respective places and houses. But from today it is by order of the Japanese Government that you all who are not helping the Government are to be interned. Thus you are interned according to war regulations ordered by the ruling Government. Nevertheless I promise you the following:

1. The Government will supply you with food.
2. You are to take care of your own health and any necessary assistance will be given.
3. You are to be gentle and to live peaceful among yourselves.
4. From 3.00 to 5.00 pm Tokio time you must keep to your room and be quiet.
5. You are not allowed outside the fence.
6. You are not allowed to listen to the radio.
7. You are not allowed to speak and/or communicate with outsiders.
8. You must obey your house-master who will be appointed by me.
9. The house-master may go to the market between 9 o'clock am and 12 o'clock noon Tokio time.
10. You must salute anyone wearing a Japanese uniform.

> Remember that you are interned according to war regulations;
> therefore you are to obey the orders of the government as well as myself.

BY EARLY 1942, the Japanese had succeeded in occupying a vast territory of some two million square kilometres that was filled with an incredible mix of people. About 100,000 were white Dutch, 200,000 Indo-European 'mixed race' from marriages between Dutch men and Indonesian women, 1.2 million Chinese and sixty million natives of countless local tribes who would later, after the establishment of the Indonesian Republic, become the Indonesians. Most of these natives were Muslim and many of the tribes had been longing to throw off the yoke of Dutch oppression.

Besides the establishment of the Greater East Asia Co-Prosperity Sphere, the Japanese had as a second target the liberation of the colonised peoples of East Asia, and this was an important part of Japanese war propaganda. At first, the Indonesians-to-be welcomed them, but soon some of them changed their opinion. One nationalist recalled: "We started to hear the first stories from Indonesian workers who had been sent to Burma and Thailand and the like. Stories about the terrible conditions and the many deaths. And suddenly you'd think: Listen, we have to get rid of both the Dutch and the Japanese, and we should never be dependent on foreigners again."[30]

In the first months of the occupation, everyone had to be registered. For those of mixed race, this involved establishing the percentage of their 'Dutchness'. Officially they were Dutch, but some felt more affinity with their Indonesian relatives. There were also local people who were loyal to the Dutch. Many Moluccans and Menadonese served in the KNIL, and if they managed to escape capture they joined the resistance groups that were soon formed throughout the archipelago.

The internment of Allied civilians in Indonesia, as elsewhere in East Asia, was carried out in order to isolate them from contact with Japan's enemies and in retaliation for the internment of the Japanese living in Western countries. These camps differed from those set up by the Nazis in Europe to remove real or perceived enemies of the state from society in that they never were intended to be extermination camps, even though there were rumours that orders for extermination had been given (but not carried out) towards the end of the war.

The Japanese authorities tried to eliminate Dutch influences in the Dutch East Indies entirely. They introduced the Japanese calendar, Japanese time, the Japanese flag, Japanese national holidays and the Japanese word for Japan: Nippon. The population had to bow to the Japanese flag and salute Japanese soldiers. It was forbidden to use Dutch and English; the official language became Malay, and schoolchildren had to learn Japanese.

*Bowing for the Jap. (AJF Gogelein)*[19]

Some Japanese customs were difficult to master – the formal bow, for example. An eye witness recalled:

> Everyone was told that from now on they had to bow deeply to every Jap, no matter what his rank. You had to bow so deeply that your back would be completely horizontal. If they didn't think you did it well enough they would beat you.

The ritual character of the correct bow by prisoners had a special meaning and was not intended to be a humiliation, although the Europeans felt it like that. Any protest by the prisoners was taken to be a lack of gratitude and respect to the Japanese Emperor, and this insult was severely punished. The Dutch masters had now become slaves. This loss of 'face', observed by the erstwhile servants, was a contributing factor to the demise of Dutch colonial power after the war.

# FIRST TASTE OF CAPTIVITY

EARLY IN THE occupation of Medan, the Japanese asked the various directors and administrators of local companies to continue their work in order to keep the local economy going. The Dutch men at first refused, not wanting to aid the enemy in any way. It threatened to become a dangerous situation that was defused through the mediation of the representative of the Dutch government. He informed the men that the government allowed them to continue their work which would help to keep the companies in good shape for the future.

Those working men were still allowed limited freedom of movement. They were often accompanied by a Japanese supervisor, and had to wear a white strip of cloth with a large red ball (the symbol of the rising sun, as depicted on the Japanese flag) around their upper arm. They could keep their families together and were reasonably housed, at least in the beginning of the occupation. These men were given the rather derogatory name of 'Nipponworkers' or 'ball boys' by their countrymen who were less privileged.

Henk, who had never been conscripted into the Dutch army because he was blind in one eye, belonged to these Nipponworkers. He had a special pass

*Henk's 'Nipponworker' pass.*

(*Soerat keterangan* is Indonesian for identity certificate) that allowed him to travel around. "I was never sure what would happen when I showed that pass," he recalled years later. "Sometimes the Japs would be quite polite, even salute and let me through without problems, but at other times they yelled at me and hit me in the face with open hand, but then let me through anyway."

During the first months of the occupation, Henk spent eight weeks working on a plantation in Siantar. Rie was briefly interned in Tandjoeng Merawa and Kampong Baroe. In November 1942, they were reunited in so-called family internment at the St Jozefschool. This had been a boarding school for boys before the war but now whole families were packed together in classrooms, living on mattresses on the floor. Some privacy was created by hanging sheets between the mattresses. In this unlikely place and at this inopportune time, they conceived their first child.*

The time came when Rie was told she had to move to the women's camp at Poeloe Brayan. The Japanese commander himself came to tell her, saying he was sorry. This commander, Oyama, was a kind and gentle man who had arranged for Rie to have extra rations because she was pregnant. Now he told her he would get her proper transport. He phoned the hospital to come with an ambulance, because he had a pregnant woman, about to deliver, who had to be moved. Rie recalled later: "He was very nervous, came to my room all the time, shouting at me so that everyone thought he was furious with me. He showed me how to walk, with my belly far out and to tell the nurse that I was ten days away from delivery."

The ruse obviously worked for a lady in the camp mentioned in a letter to her husband that the Japanese at the school had been angry when they found out about the pregnancy. This same lady** recounts Rie's arrival in camp Poeloe Brayan D on 2 July 1943:

> Friday afternoon Rie Jongbloed arrived here from the St Jozefschool.
> Note well: with 25 *collies barang*. Her arrival had not been announced.
> Therefore she had to be fitted in somewhere in a hurry. Because someone
> had left from our room, we had to make place for her. You'll understand
> that we, however much *kasian* we had with Rie, were far from
> enthusiastic. An eight months pregnant woman was not exactly suitable
> for our small children. We could hardly protest because after all Rie is
> a nice gal who you don't want to hurt. Any protest might have been
> explained wrongly. Mrs van Genderen [the camp leader] finally brought

---

* One wonders that this could happen, all things considered. They must have gone about it like hedgehogs – very carefully.
** Gini Drijvers in a letter published in a compilation of various diaries and letters called *Noord Sumatra in Oorlogstijd* (*North Sumatra during the war*)[21].

the *hantjo*. The outcome: *tida bisa, lima tjoekoep* – not possible, five is enough. So that problem was solved. She has now moved in with Mrs Lötscher* in a *goedang* downstairs. That is better. After having been here for two days she moved yesterday.

How Rie could have had that much luggage is amazing. After all, she had been allowed only two *collies barang* when she left her house in April 1942. It can only be assumed that Henk, during the time when he had relative freedom of movement as a Nipponworker, had been able to collect possessions from their house or to buy stores of food and items for barter.

The remarkable Japanese commander Oyama once warned Henk that the military police were about to confiscate all the belongings of the prisoners and told him to hide some valuable items. Apparently he was more used to Western people because had lived in the United States for a long time, possibly as a spy. He liked to help.

A week earlier Henk had lost his freedom when he was detained in Soekamoelia prison in Medan. Somehow the Japanese had found out about Overakker's secret orders and knew there were instructions for post-war leadership hidden somewhere in Medan. They were especially incensed over this because it assumed that the Japanese would lose the war – this was still far from certain in mid-1943. They did not exactly know where it was or who knew about it and imprisoned several men for interrogation. "The day before yesterday W..., H..., K... and Jongbloed were taken from the Jozefschool, probably in relation with the same matter," Giny Drijvers' husband wrote to her on 26 June 1943.

While this roundup of suspects is documented in letters and diaries, the exact reason for it is not mentioned, except that the Japanese had concluded that money went from the Europeans to the secret effort to establish post-war

---

* Lotte Lüsschen

authority. They therefore interrogated anyone who had the opportunity to transport money.

Henk talked about his ordeal in Soekamoelia only a little. He said: "Some people cracked, but I could never blame them, for it was very difficult to hold out when the Japs carried out their interrogations."

He was in prison for five months. More than once in later life, he commented that his year of solitary confinement had been unbelievably hard. Normally he did not tend to exaggerate. Undoubtedly, it had seemed like a year to him.

Henk's cell was a hot, damp room without even a mat or mattress to sleep on. He lost weight rapidly because the daily rations he was given were minimal. Soon sleep became difficult because of the pressure of bones on concrete. He still had a handkerchief and folded this into a small square that he could use as a pad under his hipbone. He might well have died in that cell except for a small act of human kindness. Often at night, a small saucer with rice and water was pushed into his cell underneath the door. One moonlit night, he managed to see that his unknown benefactor was a Japanese soldier. Henk always felt this man was an angel that God had sent to save his life.

Among Henk's prison wardens was an Indian Sikh. One day this man came into his cell and said he wanted to tell him something. He said that Henk need not fear the impending prisoner transport to Formosa because he would not be going on it. This could have been common knowledge but the following certainly was not. He told Henk that his wife was pregnant with a girl, that all three of them would survive the war and that a son would be born after the war. He also said that the family would live in North America later on.

Memory plays tricks. Henk often remarked later that he did not know that his wife was pregnant when they were separated, until this prison warden told him about the pregnancy. Rie must have conceived in November 1942, no doubt in the joy of their reunion after several months of separate confinement.

Somehow the numbers don't tally. Rie may not have been aware of a pregnancy immediately, either because she did not menstruate because of partial starvation, or due to her earlier almost total ovarectomy. Still, by the end of June, when Henk was taken to prison, she must have been visibly pregnant.

The Sikh's predictions turned out to be correct. The prisoner transport to Formosa left a few days later without Henk. It was torpedoed and there were few survivors. Rie delivered the daughter that Henk did not see until the day after her second birthday. His son was born eleven months after their postwar reunion. And when his children were teenagers, the family lived in Canada for a few years.

Henk was released from prison in the first week of November 1943 and interned in the men's camp at Sungei Sengkol.

## 6

# LIFE IN POELOE BRAYAN

POELOE BRAYAN, THE women's camp where Rie was first interned, was only a ten-minute drive away from Sungei Sengkol, Henk's first camp. Poeloe Brayan consisted at first of Camp A, B and C, a settlement of labourer's huts and *pondoks* or *hongs*, buildings of woven bamboo with a palm leaf roof. Inside, wooden or bamboo platforms lined the walls and on these platforms the women were allocated a ninety centimetre wide area as their living space. Up to two hundred women and children occupied each *pondok*. Later, a Camp E was created, and this camp soon gained a reputation for being particularly terrible, mainly because of its low-lying location, which caused flooding with every rain.

Camp D on the other hand – where Rie found herself in the summer of 1943 – had stone houses, a group of four double-storey houses in the centre surrounded by a road, with another dozen houses facing this road on the perimeter. The total surface area was about four hundred by six hundred metres. Originally the compound had been created as housing for the staff of the railway, the DSM. The station lay just outside the surrounding fence.

Although the houses in themselves were better than the *pondoks* of the other

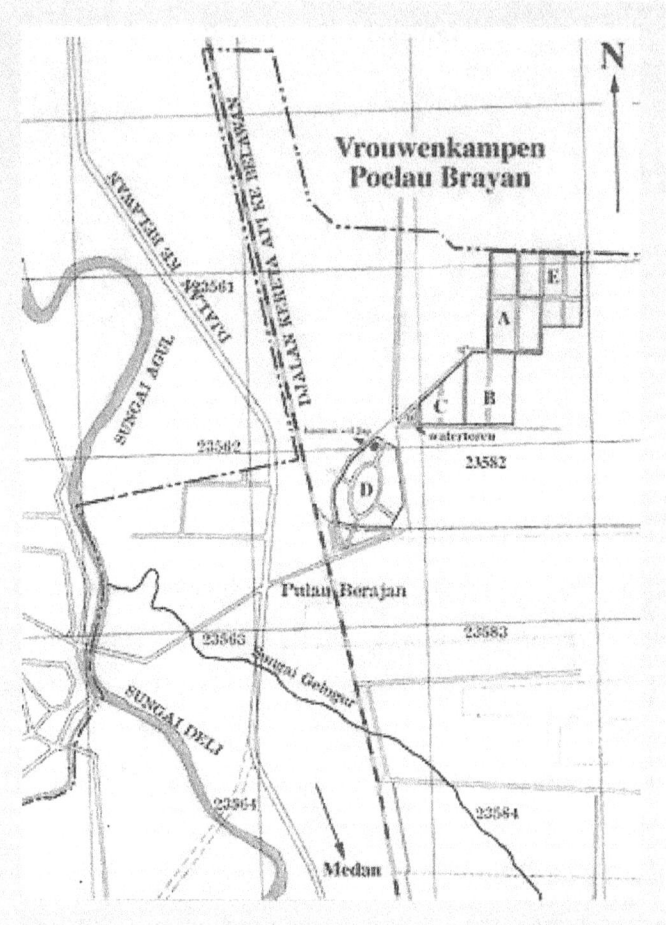

*The five camps of Poeloe Brayan, north of Medan.*

four camps, they were crammed so full of people that life was barely tolerable. By the time Rie entered the camp, there were more than five hundred women and children living there. Each room held up to eight people and in one house more than sixty people had to share one bathroom and one toilet.

In a TV documentary of interviews with people who were children during those war years, one ex-detainee of another camp said: "We were eighty-five people in a four-room house. People even slept in the kitchen cupboards....

The biggest problem for me was that you could never ever be alone anywhere."29

The smells in the camps must have been mostly bad ones: stagnant water in the ditches, open latrines, dirty bodies, damp clothing, mouldy possessions, cockroaches, bed lice... smells more usually associated with city slums or the huddled huts of poor *kampongs* in the countryside.

Indonesian houses usually had a *kakilima,* a covered corridor, around the house, sometimes leading to a number of servants' quarters and *goedang* storerooms. Rie was allocated one of these small rooms, a space of about four

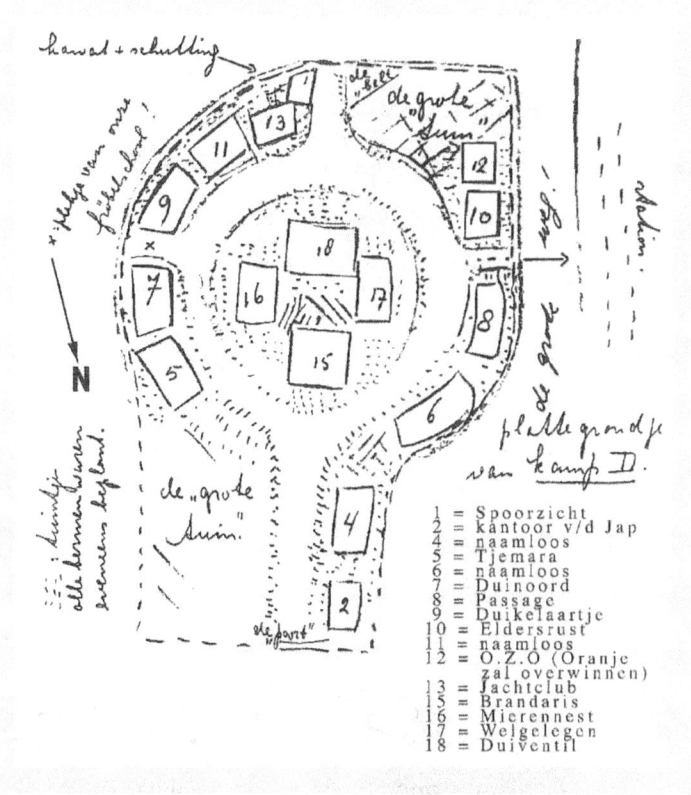

*Poeloe Brayan D. Rie and her baby lived in the servants' quarters of house number 17.*

and a half square metres, for herself and her baby, so compared with others she was well off, having some privacy and relative quiet.

The internees were free to choose their own camp committees that were charged with the execution of the orders issued by the Japanese. Each house had a 'housemother' and the whole camp was represented to the Japanese camp commander by their camp leader. There is no evidence that these camp functionaries were democratically chosen, at least not in the women's camps; they were likely either appointed or volunteered. It took courage to be the camp leader because the Japanese were fickle and leaders needed great diplomacy to convey the needs and wishes of the women. Any breach of the Japanese rules could result in a beating for the camp leader. In addition, the women whom they had to represent were not always appreciative and criticised their leaders more often than they thanked them. The medical doctors also played an important role in the communication with the Japanese. They had to fight for better living conditions, especially concerning hygiene.

In Poeloe Brayan D there was a central kitchen. While this relieved the women from the daily chores of putting meals together, the kitchen duties that had to be taken in turn were often extremely heavy and unpleasant. Of course, with outside temperatures being constantly in the mid-thirties centigrade (mid-nineties Fahrenheit) the heat of the cooking fires must have been quite unbearable.

In the beginning the cooking stoves were no more than oil drums in which wood fires were stoked; later, stone stoves were built. However, wood remained the only fuel available, and was the bane of the kitchen workers. The wood was often bad and most of the time wet, and had to be chopped to usable size with very dull axes – no easy task for the women. To keep fires alight, girls were assigned to *kipas* the flames with fans of woven bamboo. The smoke was so intense that these teenagers constantly had inflamed eyes in soot-black faces.

The various duties were cooking porridge, rice, vegetables and running the diet kitchen. The latter was the place where special soft food was cooked for those suffering from dysentery and where other special food requirements were taken care of.

Whereas normally a kitchen in the tropics would give out the most delicious smells of hot oils, garlic, curry, onions and *trassi*, the shrimp paste that features in almost every dish, the camp kitchens could only make rather bland food, because salt, pepper and spices were only delivered once in a while. Sugar was a rarity too. Taste had to be imagined. In a way it was good that the food did not smell so good, for in that way it did not stimulate an appetite that would not be satisfied.

All supplies had to be hauled from the Japanese headquarters in the neighbouring ABC camp to the kitchen so there were carrying duties: wood for the fires, thirty kilo sacks of rice and corn, piles of sweet potatoes, small amounts of fish and sometimes vegetables. What was provided by the Japanese was often of poor quality and never sufficient, so the women planted vegetable gardens on every scrap of soil between and around the houses. These vegetable plots required hoeing. Every adult in the camp spent several hours a day on this chore. The plots were fertilised by hand with manure from the cesspits.

On a par with this unpleasant activity were the compulsory *parit* duties. The camp was surrounded by two rows of barbed wire, or *kawat*, fences with a ditch in between. This *parit* had to be cleaned constantly, with the women standing ankle deep in oozing mud with their bare feet and often sore-covered legs. But *parit* duty had an advantage: you could gather the snails and slugs that proliferated between the weeds and cook them for a much-needed protein supplement.

Schooling was organised for the children, so some women had teaching duties. And from time to time there were periods in which the Japanese ordered the women to do special chores for them. Rie listed: 'sew mattress covers and shirts, twist rope, make envelopes, fill mattresses, and embroider stars'. In the later camp, at Aek Pamienke, they also had to make coffins, dig graves and bury the dead, dig the latrines and empty them.

Apart from all these duties, the women had to keep their quarters clean – no easy task in such overcrowded spaces. Washing their clothes was difficult without soap. No wonder the women were usually so tired at the end of the day that there was little interest in social gatherings and any kind of further education – activities that were far more prevalent in the men's camps – although apparently the young girls in the camp performed plays and musicals at times. The detainees faithfully attended church services and observed the national holidays.

A strange contradiction in the camps was that although everyone was supposed to have given their money and valuables to the Japanese, there was still the possibility of buying extra food from them. The items that were ordered were delivered at the Japanese command post in the ABC camp, then had to be hauled to the kitchen, from where they were distributed to the houses and then to the people who had paid for them. In the early days of internment, local food-hawkers were allowed inside the camp to sell their wares, but by mid-1943 this privilege had obviously been forbidden as Rie's diary makes no mention of it.

In a way, money helped unite internees. Within the camp there were women who had a lot of money, and others who had none. In order to create more equality, the rich contributed to a camp fund that then provided the have-nots with some pocket money to spend on their personal necessities.

What money couldn't buy from the Japanese still had to be acquired. As less and less food was provided, the practice of smuggling became more important. In Poeloe Brayan, it consisted mainly of contacting local people on the outside and offering them barter items in return for food. Textiles were particularly valuable as the war had stopped their import and there was no

*Kitchen in one of the camps. (Joke Broekema)*[19]

local manufacturing. White sheets were popular with the Muslims who used them to bury their dead. Those who, like Rie, had relatively large amounts of barter goods, were able to obtain some much-needed sugar, fat or dried fish.

Very little is mentioned about the smuggling activities in letters and diaries. No one risked spelling out the smuggling routes and methods for fear that the Japanese would find that information during one of their frequent surprise house searches. In Poeloe Brayan, it seems to have been mainly the adolescent boys who were involved in the smuggling. Several were caught and taken to prison, where they had to stand trial.[23] While in custody they suffered beatings, hunger and discomfort in crowded cells. After they were given sentences of several years' imprisonment, they were usually returned to the internment camps.

Small children posed another problem for the camp. The central kitchen received only half an adult ration of food per child. Food was distributed in equal portions per person, so this meant that in the early days when there were still many small children around, the women's camps consistently received less food than the men's camps. In fact there was a constant need to provide supplementary food.

Camp D had electricity and in the beginning the women were able to cook extra vegetables or heat up cold food using electric hot plates or the flat bottoms of irons. Later this was forbidden and all electrical appliances were confiscated. Then the women used charcoal in small wrought-iron *anglo* cookers. This posed a problem for the women who lived on the second floors of the houses, because cooking inside was forbidden as a fire precaution and they had no covered area to use their little stoves. The *kakilimas*, where in the beginning cooking on *anglos* was possible, were later closed off with planks to create more space for the ever-increasing numbers of interned women and children. Cooking out in the open was only possible during the dry season.

Fortunately in this camp the water from the taps was drinkable. Later, in Aek Pamienke camp in the jungle, water came from polluted wells and had to be boiled before use. Rie and her toddler were among detainees transferred to that camp in April 1945 and therefore had to endure only a few months there, which was just as well because the conditions at Aek Pamienke were so bad that they could not have survived much longer.

Despite being deprived of normal means of communication, detainees kept abreast of the progress on the war fronts both in Europe and in the Far East, as the regular updates in some of their diaries show. It leads to the conclusion that there must have been one or more radios hidden in the camp: the codeword 'Loet' appears to refer to this. However, rumours were rife and more often than not false, and the unrest that they caused upset the camp routine and made things even more difficult at times. Sometimes news arrived that was correct: already on 8 June 1944 the women in Poeloe Brayan knew about the invasion of France that had happened two days earlier.

Contact with the husbands was maintained by 'wire' – which in this case meant smuggled letters thrown across the barbed wire *kawat* or carried by loyal erstwhile servants or office employees. If the mail was intercepted, the whole camp was punished.

# Chapter 7

# TERROR AND TEDIUM

THE GOVERNING OF Sumatra, including the daily running of the internment camps, was at first in the hands of Japanese civilians. These were not the worst people to deal with, because they did not impose too many rules or interfere much with the camp activities. There was some military presence in each camp and organisation, but this was kept to a minimum because the soldiers and officers were needed for the continuing war effort. To help with guard duties, local men were given jobs as so-called *soekarillas* – volunteer local soldiers. They were widely disliked and distrusted as they enjoyed seeing their former 'masters' humiliated and in distress. Also they needed to impress their new masters, the Japanese. Most feared were the military police, the *kenpeitai*,* whose members, the *kenpei*, carried out interrogations, tortures and executions.

Only later, when the tide of war turned, did a military administration take over in Java and Sumatra as they were considered front-line regions. Then the civilian detainees became *de facto* prisoners of war.

The scale of the Japanese internment operation was huge. On Sumatra

---
* Often wrongly called the *kempetai*.

alone, 12,000 Dutch men, women and children were interned as well as about five hundred other nationalities, including British and Australians. Very few Eurasians were interned with the Western civilians in the Dutch East Indies, unlike in the other conquered countries of the Far East.

The Japanese army did not allow observers from neutral countries such as Switzerland and Sweden, or from the Red Cross, to visit internment camps under its control for fear of espionage.

Although the Geneva Conventions forbade conquering and occupying powers to use prisoners of war and detainees as slave labour, it was a rule conveniently forgotten when it suited those in command. The men in the last main camp of Sumatra (Si Rengo Rengo) had to work plots of land to grow vegetables for the Japanese staff. Those of the men who were still strong enough did the work without protest, welcoming it as a change from the pervading boredom of camp life.

This could not be said of the prisoner of war camps that were under military command from the beginning. Most of the POWs captured in Sumatra were put to work on development projects like the Pakan Baroe railway, which was started in May 1944. Crossing the island of Sumatra, this railway was 220 kilometres long and was built so the Japanese would not have to ship precious oil and other resources necessary for their war effort through oceans controlled by the Allies.

While much has been published about the harsh conditions endured by the POWs working on the 'Death Railway' in Burma, the miseries of those forced to work on the less well-known Sumatran death railway were just as real. Tens of thousands of local labourers, called *romushas*, and around five thousand American, British, Dutch and Australians, the ABDA prisoners of war, were forced to work on the Pakan Baroe railway. These two groups both had distinct jobs in the construction and rarely came into contact with each other. The Indonesian 'slaves' made the *talus*, or road bed, shifting soil and building dykes through marshes. The Westerners collected the wooden sleepers and iron rails from depots and transported them to the front of the bed. The Westerners were not young men like those on the Burma railroad. The average age of the Dutch contingent, for instance, was thirty-six years. This undoubtedly had an impact on the survival rate. Many died.

One survivor, Engineer Meijer, called it "a time of utter misery". Recording his memories of working on the Sumatran death railway, he wrote:[30] "I can't remember a single smile during the final six months. The Japs didn't only want to build a railway, they also wanted as many people as possible to die in the process. They succeeded very well. Sometimes you would return from the railway to discover that another friend had died. You only went to Camp 2, the camp for the ill, to die."

Another ex-prisoner described his first day:[20]

"*Kiotskei*! Forwards, march!" To the harbour. Endless heaps of rails and sleepers. Cockerill-Krupp, coming from demolished railroads in Atjeh, Deli and Malacca. We have to load them. No one is used to this heavy work, our bones groan. We clamber onto the wagons, we carry beams of ten meters length, six of us on our naked shoulders. Iron with a weight of 300 kilograms is carried across stumps and through potholes to the *talus*. Hour after hour the Jap harasses us in the burning sun. There is enough for hundreds of kilometers. My back is breaking, my loins snap. No water is given. My tongue sticks to my palate. Dizzy with thirst and effort I lean against a tree for a minute. Like a fury the guard jumps at me and hits me on my head with a piece of wood. Blood drips from my ears. ...

Pause. It is one o'clock. Line up for the lunch that consists of water. A relief.

For a long time the sun stands at its zenith, a fire-spitting volcano that burns us alive. Deep apathy comes over me, I don't feel any hunger, any thirst, any pain and any exhaustion any more. A mindless machine, working mechanically.

After a long workday we drag our paralysed bodies to the shed. We have borne the load and the heat of the day and now the reward is waiting for us at home. A handful of rice, decorated with a few leaves of boiled oebi-leaves, tough as parchment.

The railway could also be blamed for many thousands of deaths at sea. On 26 June 1944, 176 Dutch POWs died when the *Harukiku Maru*, a three thousand ton steamer previously named the *Van Waerwijck* before it was seized by the Japanese, was torpedoed and sunk by the HMS *Truculent*, one hundred kilometres southeast of Medan. The men were being transported to the railway.

An even worse disaster occurred when a transport ship, the *Junyo Maru*, carrying thousands of POWs and *romushas* was torpedoed on 18 September 1944 by the HMS *Tradewind*. The figures for the number of dead of this disaster vary wildly: from 5,500 to 7,400. Most were *romushas* who could not swim. Those who survived the initial impact and the maelstrom created by the sinking ship found themselves in the company of frenzied sharks attracted by the bloody turmoil. A Japanese corvette escorting the *Junyo Maru* initially only picked up Japanese survivors, but returned later to take care of the prisoners. Survivors painted a terrible picture of what went on in those dawn hours before the coast of Sumatra.[20]

Rafts were spread across an immense surface. In the middle of a concentration of debris, trunks and rafts the boat stopped. A few yellow figures raise a white cloth with the red ball. White guys, burned bright red, dogpaddle towards us. The Japs rage and yell at their audacity.

Whoever comes too close is killed, whoever gets hold of the boat has his hands chopped off. Everything is focused on saving the Japs, only then the others get a chance. We pull aboard a young coolie, whose right leg has been amputated by a shark. The poor boy threatens to bleed to death. One of us, a nurse, begs the Jap for a piece of rope to use as a tourniquet. Nothing doing. Back into the water with him.

The 680 POWs and two hundred *romushas* who were saved ended up in the camps of the railway, where dozens did not survive.

In a moment of supreme irony, the last spike on the railway – gold coloured in the tradition of major rail links – was hammered into place by a Japanese officer during a small ceremony on the 15 August 1945, the day of the unconditional Japanese surrender. In his speech, he said:

Now the railway is finished, thanks to all your efforts. I have the honour to announce in the name of His Highness the Emperor of Japan, that all of you will be given a rest. Shortly you will be transported to a better place. And from today the rations of rice, vegetables and meat will be increased. You will receive these new rations as soon as we receive fresh stock. At this moment we don't have meat or vegetables and only rice for a few days. While waiting for transport, you are not permitted to leave the camp.

That was all. No word about a capitulation or the end of the war.

The railway would never be used by the Japanese. In fact, it was never used by anyone, mainly because the construction was of exceptionally bad quality. Sabotage by the POWs rendered the railway even worse than its lack of design had managed to achieve.

The railway workers did not hear about the end of the war until the end of

August. Even then they had to remain inside the camp under slightly improved conditions until the Allied troops reached their remote area to liberate and repatriate them. The British and American POWs were repatriated immediately, but the Dutch waited until November. The last POWs left the camps on 25 November 1945.

Statistically, the Pakan Baroe railway is a stark reminder of the brutalities of the war in the East. More than thirty-seven per cent of the 6,600 POWs shipped to Sumatra to build this rail link died, either during transport or while toiling on the construction. The death toll among the *romushas* was much higher – figures given differ but it is certain that more than 80,000 of them perished in connection with the Pakan Baroe railway. This one project accounted for thirty to forty per cent of the estimated 200,000 to 250,000 *romushas* in total who died at the hands of the Japanese during the war.

IN THE CIVILIAN camps, the conditions were fortunately never so dire. All camps were different, both because of their geographical location and in how they were run by the Japanese command as well as by the detainees themselves. For instance, the mountain camp of Brastagi had a cooler climate and no mosquitoes, but women held there had less contact with the outside world and the conditions in general were very difficult. The camps in the greater Medan area provided more opportunities for smuggling food and other necessities as well as the letters that kept the detainees in contact with family members in other camps. Letters were smuggled mainly by loyal ex-servants among the locals, or by the few women who had passes to go outside – the doctors, for instance. For a while in Medan, detainees had the rare opportunity to visit dental clinics or hospitals in town. Sometimes husbands and wives managed to get appointments at the same time for the sole purpose of seeing each other briefly. Officially, the only contact that was allowed between the camps was via pre-printed cards that had to be filled out in

*The well at Sungei Sengkol. (G v d Meulen)*[21]

English or Malay. Occasional Red Cross notes to the family back in Holland were sent, but of course no one knew if they ever arrived

AFTER HENK WAS released from prison in November 1943, he was first interned in camp Sungei Sengkol, southwest of Medan. This camp, housed in a hospital and its satellite buildings, was 'home' to about 650 men and boys. Initially only boys older than fourteen were grouped with the men, but in the last year of the war boys of ten years old were sent to the men's camps. Even before then, mothers sometimes sent their younger sons to the men's camps so that they might join their fathers and get more food: in the men's camps everyone, irrespective of age, got a full ration.

Henk's letters suggest that in general the food situation in Sungei Sengkol was not too bad. The diet was monotonous but the rations were sufficient to

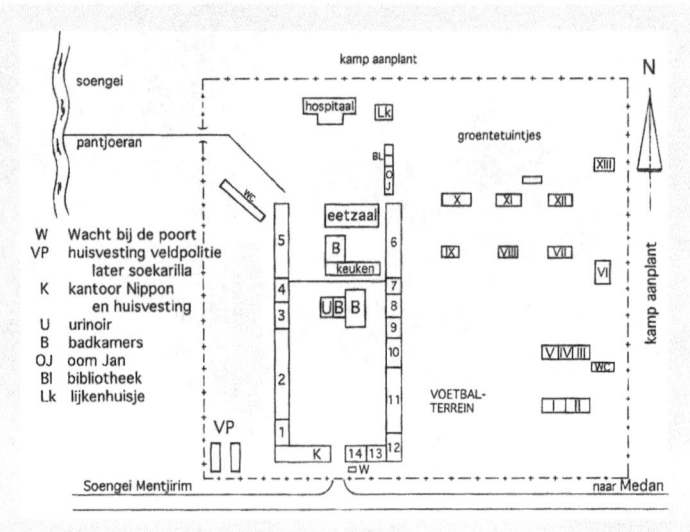

*Camp Sungei Sengkol. Henk's hut was one of the two by the eastern fence.*

keep the men active and healthy. Unfortunately that situation changed for the worse as the war dragged on and new camps were established.

Camp Sungei Sengkol was situated on the bank of the river Sengkol. Between the camp enclosure and the river, a washing place called a *pantjoeran* had been created. To get there, the men were allowed to leave the fenced area. This they also did, under Japanese supervision, to work on a large *oebi* plantation, where the sweet potatoes that supplemented the rations were grown, and to cut trees for firewood in the surrounding forest. Of course, every time the men broke the strict camp rules, the Japanese revoked these privileges.

In their attempts to make life as normal as possible in Sungei Sengkol, the detainees set up schooling for teenage boys. They attended classes and were even taking exams and receiving certificates. Later it became more difficult due to a lack of materials and the general apathy of the prisoners caused by starvation. One of those boys, Frits Looman, described the situation well in texts quoted at the Dutch Resistance Museum:[30]

We were taught in the dining hall in an open shed in the middle of the camp. Groups of six or seven boys would sit around each table. We didn't have any books. Everything was dictated: rows of words, chemistry, etc. My notebook shows that in 1943 we were given a French dictation exercise about daily life in the camp. We were taught until we were transferred to Camp Si Rengo Rengo. The conditions there were so awful that we didn't do anything any more.

Another boy, Ernest Hillen, talked about the boredom he experienced as a young boy in a women's camp:9

...the worst thing about living in Bloemenkamp was not the heat, fear, smells, noise, flies, too many bodies, too little food, scratches that festered, and diarrhea – it was the sameness. The days and weeks and months had dragged by... It was even a relief, it seemed sometimes, that there were always new no-nos: no lights on after eight, no wood-gathering for cooking fires, no meeting in groups, absolutely no *gedekking* [smuggling] through the wall; on and on.

Detainee Robert Rouveroy van Nieuwaal[31] was deployed, with a friend, to take care of sick men in Camp Sungei Sengkol, with some unexpected consequences:

One man gave us a book on how to build a crystal radio set to thank us. With great difficulty, we built a radio. The Japanese shouldn't know about it. We stole the necessary materials from a storage shed. The barbed wire on the fencing acted as the antenna. It worked! The radio allowed us to listen to the Allied broadcasts of Radio Colombo.

The radio only received Morse code, not speech, but it worked fine at certain times during the night, Bob recalled later.

For young boys, life in Sungei Sengkol was not always unpleasant. They were free, often without supervision, did not have to spend much time 'in school' and were able to have adventures. Many of these adventures were aimed at improving the food or firewood situation. They kept chickens and ducks (one boy's diary consists almost entirely of a record of the number of eggs that his two ducks laid), they dismantled wooden structures and they smuggled. If they were caught in this latter activity, they were taken to prison for punishment, but often returned to the camp after a week or so.

One boy, who came from another camp where conditions were reportedly much worse, remarked: "The Sungei Sengkol camp was a vacation camp." That comment earned him a lot of criticism from former inmates, but he explained that because of the camp's location and size, the fences were not visible all the time and you did not have the feeling of being shut in. For him, the main advantage of being in the camp was that he now had his father's undivided attention. Whereas before the war his father had been busy and was not easily accessible, they now slept side by side and had time to talk, at length and about everything. He said: "I could hardly contain my happiness."[13]

In both the men's and the women's camps, people established working relationships which were called *kongsis*. Members of a *kongsi* took care of one another in times of sickness or bereavement, shared their food and other belongings and developed close relationships that often lasted for the rest of their lives. In a strange coincidence, Henk's best friend in the camps was a surgeon, whose wife was a member of Rie's *kongsi*. It was she who took care of the baby when leg ulcers forced Rie to spend many weeks in hospital, unable to walk.

Although the men had plenty of duties to keep them occupied during the daytime, they seemed to have had more energy left to pursue other activities at night and during their time off. Sungei Sengkol had a choir, a drama group, weekly lectures on all sorts of topics, church services and classes. Henk told his wife that he was studying a variety of subjects, reading and also teaching a course. "We can't just take and give nothing," he reasoned.

*Sleeping area in men's hong at Sungei Sengkol.*
*(G v d Meulen)* [21]

# ೞೞೞ 8 ಙಙಙ

# EVEN NOW, NEW LIFE

IT WAS A SMUGGLED letter, a tiny packet of tightly folder paper no more than two centimetres square, that Rie received in the middle of August from Henk, who was still in prison. On the outside, in the unmistakable handwriting of her husband, was written:

To M.C.A. Jongbloed-Ochel
(to be opened after the delivery)
When the pain and suffering of the birth are behind you and you long
for life again, then an as yet unread letter from me might be just what
you need! (John 16:21)* Henk

My dearest darling,
Oh, how I want to be with you at this moment to condense all I am going
to say into two kisses. The first one for you, the second one for our little

---

* John 16:21 – 'When a woman gives birth, she has distress because her time has come, but when her child is born, she no longer remembers the suffering because of her joy that a human being has been born into the world.'

one. For, if God has blessed the outcome, and I don't doubt that any more, then as you are reading this our little one is lying in its cradle and fortunately knows nothing of the circumstances in which it was born. My dearest treasure, I thank God and you too for this reward, so unmerited. Please know that my heart is full of joy and I am consumed by longing to be with you, forever, to help and support you.

You, my darling, have had all the difficulties all those months, the pain and the care and now you are responsible for this fragile creature, but at least you have it and you see it and you can take care of it and enjoy it and the first smile on that small wrinkled face is for you. And the little shrimp-fists will first point at you. That is your right. Maybe – and only God knows this – my share will be nothing else but to pray that both of you will be and remain healthy and that you will want for nothing. And that's what I am doing and what I'll keep doing. To our little one applies what the mother of [St] Augustin once said: 'A child of so much prayer can never be lost.' I am so curious whether it'll be a 'he' or a 'she'.

I am convinced that I, assuming that I'll still be here in two weeks' time, will not be left in uncertainty for long. The *kabar angin* works fast. LA says: a daughter. I have no preference, I find everything equally wonderful. The second kiss that you give our little one is mine. Tell it that.

Sweetheart, isn't our life taking a strange course? Like with this child. For many years we could have expected it in all peace and quiet and now, now when everything is so difficult, seems so gloomy, now God is already working for our future. This birth is witness of the fact that he has answered our prayer for a family right from the beginning. And therefore – do not worry. Pray often and do what you must do in patience and forbearance. Having done that, the fruit of justice shall appear, just as the fruit of our Love already has.

I want so much to cherish you in your childbed and to spoil you with all I can think of. But that isn't possible. Bad for you, worse for me. Be strong in the certain knowledge that I love you, as you love me. God will be your Father. I am with you in thought anyway, all day, and before you know, in reality. Bye my darling, and now also: bye my sweet little thing. Many kisses and all my love,

    Henk

Less than two weeks after his speculations the baby was born, on the name day of St Augustin. Rie started a baby book, as was customary at the time, which became a diary of her daughter's development as well as a record of their ordeal. The first entry was written about ten days later, on 7 September, after she had received the next letter from Henk. This letter contained a poem that explained the baby's name mentioned in the first entry.

On August 28th, at 4.22 pm Nippon time* our Marijcke Victoria Désirée was born.

    It was a glorious moment to hear her voice for the first time. Our baby was born in the small hospital of the internment camp Poeloe Brayan. The doctors were dr. Einthoven and dr. van der Molen, assisted by Mother Superior Esfride and the midwife Mrs Kerkhof. It was sad that her pappie was not there for bad Japs have taken him to prison.

    The baby we wanted for such a long time is a little blond girl with a pink round face and blue eyes and she weighs 7 pounds and 20 grams. She has thin strawberry blond hair. She is lying next to me in her cradle, making cosy spluttering noises. She hardly cries and drinks with gusto.

    A paragon of an internment child.

---

\* The birth certificate (see page 92) mentions 2.10 pm Medan time. Officially Sumatra's Nippon Time (NT) was 2.5 hours later than 'sun time' which upset the daily rhythm by causing work times to be in the heat of the day and mealtimes at odd hours.

Birth certificate: the father's name had been forgotten initially and was added later in the bottom corner.

Marijcke either gives a late afternoon concert or she performs at night. The audience in the hospital prefers the late afternoon concert. She drinks a lot, the third day 60 grams each time. Today, 7 days old, already 110 grams at each feeding. She has reached her birth weight already again. Every day she is allowed to cuddle with me. Her radiant eyes then look at you, passionately she sucks her fingers, at times her fist disappears completely into her mouth. She has acute hearing, because when she is crying at night and I turn around in bed, she stops immediately. When she notices that I am not coming to attend to her, she raises her voice a little bit more.

Last night she did not cry for the first time. She woke up at 4 am. I fed her and then she quietly fell asleep again. She is learning! She already has many admirers, everyone thinks she is lovely. After a week she is starting to turn into a real human being. She was given wonderful gifts, even a little apron. We earmarked that for the *oebi* duties, but maybe she will be able to use it for something else, for we'll hope that those nasty Japs will have disappeared by then.

After about 10 days our little girl is starting to look around. When she is brought to me to be fed, she opens her eyes wide and takes in everything about me, her mother. She laughs a lot in her sleep; that is when good angels float by her cradle, says the nurse.

After a long wait we finally heard something from pappie. That was wonderful, wasn't it Marijcke? She seemed to be extra good. There was a poem and a letter for Marijcke from her father.

Henk's letter was dated 30 August. The *kabar angin* had worked fast indeed. One can only imagine the happiness that inspired him to write thirteen verses of poetry, two of which are included here: *

* The whole poem in its original Dutch can be found in Appendix B.

*Voor Marijcke – Jes. 21: 12a*

*Jij bent voor ons de morgenstond*
*Maar ach, het is nog nacht!*
*Hoe goed dat Hij je tot ons zond,*
*Bij Hem toch is de macht.*

*Marijcke Victoria Désirée*
*In bitterheid ben je gekomen*
*De zege breng je echter mee*
*en verlangensvervulling onzer dromen.*

For Marijcke – Isa 21:12a*

For us you are the light of day
Alas, it is still night!
It's good that He sent you to us
For His is the power and might.

Marijcke Victoria Désirée
In bitterness you were born
But the victory you bring,
The fulfilment of our desires.

'Father, I thank you' was the first and the only thing I could utter when I heard about your arrival, Marijcke. The first thing, because God has wanted to give you to us, although we have not deserved such a great happiness. The only thing because tears of happiness

---

\* Isaiah 21:11-12a:
'Watchman, what of the night? / Watchman, what of the night?'
The watchman replies, / 'Morning is coming, and also the night.'

and an all pervading feeling of joy made speaking and thinking impossible.

Little darling, unfortunately I cannot see you yet; that privilege is just for your dear mother for the time being, but I know what you are like! God created us in such a way that we can have close contact with one another even when we are separated.

Sleep quietly, sweet thing, 'for He shall command His angels that they keep you in all your ways' (Psalm 90). They shall carry you in their arms and one day He will bring me to you too. How wonderful that will be, the three of us together.

By 11 September, with her baby two weeks old and gaining weight, Rie had to face going back home; home "that is, to the shed where the rats are reigning at the moment. I am not looking forward to it."

When they did return, they made "a festive entry into the camp. Uncle Jap

*Handmade card from Rie's fellow detainees in Poeloe Brayan.*

allowed us to ride in a *sado* and Marijcke loved it. Our little room was full of flowers, a really great home coming. Right in front of my room there is an oil palm, and there she stays in the shade during the morning."

The first day the whole camp crowded around the cradle, but fortunately that attention waned after a few days. "Everyone is very helpful so that I can dedicate myself completely to my little girl."

Someone in Poeloe Brayan B – the 'other' camp where one of the buildings had been turned into a small hospital – had made a drawing of the baby. "We hope to be able to send it to the prison, for poor dear pappie doesn't know yet what his little girl looks like."

**September 21st [1943]**

Marijcke is starting to follow me with her eyes. From time to time she gazes at me and then a smile appears on her face. It is such a shame that pappie misses all this. Marijcke and I have settled in well again in the room in the shed. It has become a cosy little room with a wall-hanging behind the dressing table (a food chest and a cabin-trunk) and she looks with big eyes at the ducks and chicks while I dress her. Every afternoon she sits on my lap in the garden. We don't have a baby carriage but she has to have a bit of fresh air in the afternoon.

Yesterday afternoon we were sitting in the garden when we saw that nasty Jap who took our pappie away enter the camp with two soldiers, guns at the ready. Others followed and I quickly went to hide the letters from pappie. They took *tante* Zus van Gelder and two other ladies. It was terrible to see, all those armed soldiers behind them. Marijcke lay sucking her fists, unaware of all this trouble.

Every day her eyes become more focussed and she is more of a human being. This afternoon *tante* Truus Brouwer came to ask if she could have Marijcke on her lap for a moment. *Tante* Truus loved it, and

1. Kesehatan HENK and J in GOOD condition

2. Kehidoepan INTERNED IN WOMEN CAMP. FOOD ENOUGH.

3. Lain-lain 28 AUG. '43 OUR MARIJCKE VICTORIA DESIREE IS BORN. TO U.S. HENK HAS NOT YET SEEN THE CHILD. HE WAS IN PRISON, NOW IN ANOTHER CAMP. MARIJCKE IS STRONG and NICE. God save us for each other.

Rie.

*Red Cross note that Rie sent to her mother-in-law towards the end of 1943 to announce her daughter's birth.*

Marijcke no less. She lay there so sweet, looking around with her big eyes, sucking her fists and kicking her little feet.

**September 27th [1943]**
Today Marijcke and I had a real fright. We were told that our pappie would be leaving the prison and maybe even Sumatra. The cops [military police] said that the prisoners would be taken to Singapore or Formosa. We had a terrible day. Even Marijcke seemed sad. Fortunately we later got a letter from pappie, that the transfer had suddenly been cancelled. He also sent a new poem.

That letter seems to have been lost but the poem survived. It describes what Henk imagines his daughter to be like – an active, curious creature, discovering the world, who enjoys all the daily things like her bath and her food. A child that makes a fuss when she is hungry. He reassures her that no one will forget her, that she is her parents' kiss of love, their crystal of happiness. It concludes:

> Thoughts from a distance and yet near.
> I cannot yet see her but she still brings me cheer.

# 9

# 'Give me Strength'

**September 27th [1943]**
Last night Marijcke woke up early. I took care of her and put her back in her cradle, but the little girl would not have any of that. She was wide awake and wanted company. She yelled so loudly that I thought there might be a mosquito the size of an elephant in her cradle. I came out from under my mosquito netting, opened hers and immediately she was silent and a big smile curled her lips. The first time she laughed consciously. I just had to cuddle her, but after that I put her back in the cradle, in spite of her loud protest.

As the baby developed Rie had to find ways to stimulate and exercise her. They took walks around the camp every afternoon, the baby sitting on her arm for she had no pram. "Marijcke enjoys these walks immensely and she counts on them every afternoon. I am not allowed to stop, for then she starts to kick and cry. So obediently I jog around the camp twice."

They had a visitor: the Japanese commander Oyama from the St Jozefschool, who came to admire the baby. He thought she was a very sweet child and tears came to his eyes when he looked at the baby. He said he'd go to the prison to tell her father that he had a daughter. Rie did not tell him that this would be old news, for of course he was not supposed to be aware of the smuggling of letters that was going on.

> Marijcke is sweeter by the day, she has such lovely little hands and her eyes are a deep dark blue. Marijcke and I long very much for news from pappie.
>
> It is so sad to hear nothing for such a long time and it is such a pity that pappie cannot see for himself how sweetly Marijcke can smile and how she starts to make all sorts of noises.

Rie had to wait much longer for news from Henk. She even feared that the communications had stopped entirely. She was so busy with caring for the baby that she neglected herself and developed erysipelas, a very painful skin infection that should be treated with complete rest. "That is not easy with such a small child. Life in the camp is getting more difficult all the time. We get practically nothing from the Jap any more."

The harder life in the camp became, the harder it was to keep the anger in check. The general disquiet in the camp boiled over in an uprising in the other camp during which one of the women attacked a Japanese soldier. Rie's diary record of this is brief, but in another camp diary[23], written by a young woman in Camp A, which runs almost parallel to Rie's diary, this incident is described in detail and shows how brutal the Japanese could be. Apparently some smugglers had been caught, and the man from outside was being beaten up in a terrible way, when a group of women from the camp came to the Japanese command post to protest about the lack of food.

One of the doctors was in the process of politely addressing the Jap when the women saw how the poor man was being carried outside, and suddenly they started a riot. The Jap went at them with a cudgel, kicking one of them violently in her stomach. Then one of the women grabbed the stick and hit him with it, drawing blood. Another Jap grabbed a gun – the doctor and one other lady stepped forward and told him: "Go ahead, shoot."

They were not shot but taken to prison, as were a number of other women who were suspected of having hit the Jap. Finally the woman who was the culprit turned herself in. She was the mother of eight young children. Everyone thought the others would be released but that did not happen. They were kept without food or water for three days and on one of those days they had to sit on their knees with their arms crossed the entire day. Whoever faltered was kicked. Finally they were released, all except the doctor who endured daily beatings. This brave woman was fifty years old.

In spite of Rie's worries about food and her busy-ness with all the work, the baby thrived. By 16 October, at seven weeks old she already weighed almost nine and a half pounds.

MEANWHILE HENK WAS still in the Soeka Moelia Medan prison (named after the street it was situated in). In later years he mentioned that the solitary confinement, which lasted for many months, was one of the worst experiences of his life. He was regularly tortured, and often heard men from neighbouring cells being hauled away to be executed. He never knew whether he might be next. One of the poems Henk wrote there reflects his state of mind:

> For you, Lord, it's just a short while
> For me it seems centuries, that bars
> Prevent me from doing what I want
> I don't see the sun, I don't see the stars
> I only see walls that close in on me
> Helplessness and impotence
> Combine to take my breath away

O Lord, have pity on me!
Tell me what I can expect now;
I am alone with just my thoughts.
Abide with me
Speak to me in whatever tongue
A language that I may not know
But that ends with grace.
I do not want to live from grace
My own strength and effort
Are to me the things that count
Not your crucifixion, not your blood!
Grant that I may dwell in you
That your love does not condone
My unfaithfulness of the many years
That were nothing but illusions.
I searched but did not want to find.
I never let my selfishness be less.
I had eyes just for the world.
The purpose of long hours of toil
Was always just worldly pleasure
You made a mirror of my cell
You have touched my inner being
I knew it had to happen once
I knew that tears would flow
I want to surrender now
For the rest of my life I only ask
Your help and guidance
To give me strength in war.

In Poeloe Brayan, his daughter was two months old, continued to gain weight and looked "very healthy and sweet", wrote Rie. "It's a joy to look at her. This week she had on a dress for the first time." They went to see the sisters in the other camp and enjoyed being outside for a bit. "Marijcke laughs at everyone, even at the Jap, who was actually mollified." The baby hardly ever cried, she added. "When she is awake she plays with her hands or sucks her fingers. The skin of her hand is a bit damaged."

Necessity inspired Rie to potty-train her baby as soon as possible. She spent long stretches of time after every feed balancing her atop a pink potty, both held in her lap. She noted that success with potty-training the baby "makes a difference of six nappies a day, a very good thing in these days" when soap for washing was in short supply, if available at all.

Like all detainees, Rie complained of the monotony of the food, the blandness; such a contrast to the flavours and aromas of the Indonesian cuisine they had grown to love. "We often crave something tasty and spicy." A few eggs and some smuggled dried shrimps were received with joy and gratitude. Still no word from Henk.

> This week the women from the other camp were released from prison. Many men have been released but pappie is still there and fortunately he is doing all right. Oh, if only he could see our dearest little girl just once, if only the war would end soon. We long so much for a quiet life with the three of us. We pray every day that pappie will be spared for us by God!

Then came the news that Henk had been released from prison and taken to the Sungei Sengkol men's camp. Rie enthused that he was free again, which seems a strange statement, given the fact that he was still interned. She also observed that "large numbers of Japanese are coming in by train, probably from Burma, where heavy fighting is going on. Shall we be free soon? We all keep hoping!" Unfortunately there were to be another two years before that day of freedom.

Finally a letter from Henk arrived, undated, written just after his arrival in the men's camp:

> My darling,
> I am going to use this first real opportunity, both the previous little notes were extra and served only to tell you about my happy entry here. I am sure you were happy to know about it. I am too, I can assure you.
> I am only allowed to use one piece of paper.

Apparently there were various ways of getting letters from one camp to the other. Sometimes contact was allowed officially, although severe censorship would be applied. From time to time a parcel of letters was smuggled to the women's camps by the camp leaders whenever an opportunity presented itself. This could never be predicted exactly, which is why the letters had to be written quickly whenever a mail opportunity was announced. Quite often these parcels of letters were intercepted and destroyed. The most reliable way for communication between the camps was by means of privately smuggled notes, as Henk did via his loyal Sipef employee.

Henk was lucky in that he was assigned to a hut in the periphery of the Sungei Sengkol compound, where the conditions were not as crowded as in the hospital rooms of the central building.

> We are 16 in a small house at the edge of the camp and are much better off than those who have to stay in the large barracks in the middle of the camp. With Dr Ab Sm[ook], I have started making flower beds – marigolds and balsamina are in already; vegetables, *oebi*, etc. are all very useful and pleasant but a few flowers next to your pictures is cosy and necessary. ...
> Life is really quite rural. A while ago, after the evening service, I sat on the terrace of our *koelie* hut sucking my pipe, looking out across the countryside, while the last light disappeared in various hues. This

morning I *tjangkolled* our garden until I had to stop because of advanced blisters. Then I did my laundry (a.o. my prison-blanket), this afternoon I did many small tasks (clean, *djemoer*, etc.) and one and a half hours of camp duty (cutting and sawing wood). Both the first and the last jobs are heavy, so that I am quite tired now.

Before going to bed I always take a short walk by myself, sit down on a bench outside the real camp\* and concentrate completely on the two of you, our life and our future happiness, that will happen. I really feel it at the moment, in spite of missing you all day every day – a feeling that never leaves me.

While Henk pondered on his family and the future, he also worried about the problems of the present. Heavy rain caused him concern about the baby laundry, he wondered if Rie had enough clothes and other necessities to keep going. In his small *koelie* hut he created his 'home':

Yesterday I looked through my suitcases again, hung up your painting above my bed. I'll try to frame the coat of arms (N. Holland) you made and the drawing of Marijcke. Having a few of my own things around makes it cosy. My cupboard is already fixed, complete with curtain, very convenient here…. With everything I have again, I feel very rich, especially after having had almost nothing for four months. My little box was also still intact, very good… \*\*

But in a way, however weird that may sound, I sometimes think longingly of my previous residence. To be alone with your own heart,

---

\* In Sungei Sengkol the gate to the river and the sweet potato gardens was often open and obviously the men still had relative freedom of movement.

\*\* One of the two boxes with secret compartments that Henk had made when the war seemed imminent. Rie kept Henk's letters in hers; these only came to light fifty-two years later.

*The coat of arms of North Holland (where Henk was born), cross-stitched by Rie.*

however difficult, has temporary spiritual advantages. However, that thought must be condemned immediately because a true Christian has to be in the world ('I pray not that they will be taken out of the world, but that they will be kept in the world'). The day before yesterday pastor Wabb* pointed out the correct attitude in an inspiring lecture 'Christianity and personality'. It was a real man-to-man talk, the kind I like. We've had enough pussy-footing. Yes, my dear, our life is a struggle, but what a pleasure to do this together, even with the three of us.

It is typical that Henk should find something positive in his solitary prison

* The pastor was actually named Wap.

confinement. To derive spiritual growth from a period of hardship and solitude is understandable, but how honest is it to talk about deriving pleasure from a struggle – and even including a baby in that struggle. Henk was an idealist, and in the middle of the twentieth century, that is how people thought and what they believed.

Henk went on to talk about various people in the camp that he used to deal with in his working life, mentioning their names to Rie.

Plenty of friendship but still, I'll bless the day when I can leave here and we can return to the life that belongs to us. Nothing compares with that. Whatever, we'll just work hard, physically, mentally and spiritually, then time will pass quickly.

In order to keep mentally fit too, I started studying French, English, philosophy, civil law, rapid calculation (together with de Brauw) and I am reading several books.... The program is rather packed, but that is understandable. After the past months I want to do everything again.

Starting this afternoon I myself am giving a course in estate administration to assistants. For me it is a good rehearsal. I really hope that this will be my last residence in this war, because I am tired of these moves and changes. As a last phase this is okay...

Henk had no complaints about the food in Sungkei Sengkol. The portions were not large, just sufficient. The men cooked an extra pan of vegetables every day. Henk even learned to fry rice cakes and pancakes. Later he recalled that others were suspicious that he was receiving more food than they did, when in fact it was often less, because his weight stayed around the seventy kilo mark. "I do the heaviest duties and this is good for my muscles. I think I'll keep chopping and sawing wood later back home too. A really great sport!"

This tongue-in-cheek remark was no doubt intended to raise a smile on his wife's face. In fact, Henk was the proverbial couch potato, a master of delegation of unwanted tasks.

He asked many questions: was Rie fit again? Was everything well with "our little treasure"?

What a weird fatherhood, isn't it? Quite sad, though! After the description of the birth I have not heard anything more, so you can imagine that I can't wait to have the next installment. Can you still breastfeed Marijcke? I hope so. What is your life like now? No shocking events? Tell me too what your living conditions are now. Darling, till next time. In my mind I kiss your nice curls (won't you finally grow long hair to please me?), your eyes, your mouth and the tip of your nose. Hug our little girl really tight, all my love, Henk.

Rie managed to continue breastfeeding for almost nine months, which may have contributed a lot to the baby's survival. She answered his letter immediately, and sent Henk a beautiful drawing of the baby.

On 11 November, Rie returned to the other camp for a medical and baby check-up. She found the camp busier than usual because a lot of people from the St Jozefschool had arrived there. "They all admired Marijcke. The sisters were also crazy about her, she behaved so sweetly, crowed and laughed at everyone."

The moderately settled circumstances that each now found themselves in were conducive for writing, at least for Henk, whose letters started to arrive quite regularly, the next one coming just two weeks later. He introduced a system of numbering the letters in order to trace whether anything got lost. From his description of his surroundings, he might be writing from almost anywhere except a war zone.

This quiet Sunday is an ideal opportunity [to write a letter]. Although not everyone in our house is 'religious', we still observe the Sunday rest. It is now about noon sun-time, a bit cheerless below a covered sky and in our isolated corner it is pleasantly quiet. A few have gone to 'town' (into the camp) to chat, four are playing bridge and the rest are sitting reading on the veranda. I have put my table and chair on our small lawn and am really comfortable.

Comfortable but hungry, for by this time breakfast has been cancelled. Henk said, with typical understatement, "our appetite is good. Fortunately we are able to put together some sort of porridge in the morning, so that we don't have to have a completely empty stomach."

In the midst of all this, somehow Henk managed to keep up appearances, and when his effort backfired, he saw the funny side. He had "dressed... in immaculate white" for Saturday evening. It made him feel good but he "had to pay for this extravagance". On the way home in the darkness – there was no more oil for the lamps – he had slipped and fallen on the rain-soaked path. "The result was that my backside was suddenly in 'mourning'."

The letter went on to describe Sunday church services and mentioned how he liked singing in the choir as a second tenor. They were practising Christmas songs and had teamed up with the Roman Catholics for an ecumenical service at which the high school boys planned to do a nativity play. Besides the singing, Henk's passion was for reading.

The library here has about 900 books, many good ones, so for the time being I don't need any more. I still have quite a lot and the reading time is limited. Besides there is a treasure of books in private hands that we can also exchange....

There are more books here than there is time to read. Mornings and evenings are not free – the morning is for various activities (take care of firewood, washing, etc.). In the evening there is no light. Therefore, the afternoon is very full: giving and taking lessons, preparations, transcribing notes, etc. The dark hours are suitable to go have a chat with someone. Time flies and that is exactly how it should be, for we long for the day on which everything will be normal again. There are no words to express the longing that I feel to have the two of you with me again. It can only be conquered with prayer.

Henk recalled later that the best thing he had done was to take so many books into the camp. Whereas other people used their weight allowance for food, which disappeared in time, he was able to barter his books for food, and his 'capital' never diminished.

In his letter, he mentioned a gift that Rie had given him for his birthday.

I have searched and searched this week for that nice embroidered N. Holland coat of arms, my birthday present. I put it into the pocket of my shirt (you know the one, the beige one with a zip from Ma) and now it is not there any more. Would you know where it is? I hope that it hasn't been lost or stolen. I wanted to frame it.

Then he mused about their state of preparedness when they were interned. "We tried to prepare well, but now I wish that I had bought three times as much at the time. Well, I think we did what we could and had to do. For the rest we'll have to trust, but you must take care of things yourself." He worried that he had more than he needed while Rie and the baby might not have enough.

I have two mosquito nets. Did you not take one, except the big one? Is that enough? What did you put over the cradle? I also don't like the idea that I have two blankets and you only that small one. I worry about it, especially during the present cold nights with rain. Are you really not too cold? And how about clothing and other articles? Do you have sufficient of everything?

Several paragraphs followed about prayer and about religious discussions with fellow internees. It showed that matters of religion were very important to Henk. He was less strictly Reformed than his mother, but still lived very much in an atmosphere of worship and prayer. That may have helped overcome the physical longings for his wife and child.

I feel healthy and fit... The only thing is that it makes you aware all the time and in all sorts of ways of the appalling emptiness of this unnatural way of living. At times it hits you and takes your breath away. What a blessing is a family, what a blessing is good atmosphere, what a blessing is the work that was yours, what a blessing is the mutual complement of man and wife. At the moment there is no escape for the terrible tension and in one way or another that starts to tell. It is physically difficult and also very often spiritually. In any case, it is no use worrying too much about all these things. Working, with hands and head, and waiting with trust will bring it back to us.

"This past week," he wrote, "I remembered how, around this time ten years ago, we looked at each other decisively." This appears to be a reference to the moment they realised they were in love. Henk was just twenty years old then, Rie almost twenty-six.

Henk mentioned that a year earlier they had been together, hoping it would be forever. This was the time that they were re-united in family internment at the St Jozefschool after several months of separation. It was the time when Rie became pregnant. "So much happened in this year... the greatest joy and also the deepest misery. In spite of all we persevere. We live in hope and hope does not disappoint."

There was a postscript to this letter.

I just received your second letter that roamed around the camp for 3 days because they could not read the name. I had been quite sad this week when I hadn't heard anything. Stupid oafs! Please print the name clearly, from now on. Good to know that all is well with the two of you, although the general situation makes me very sad. You write again about a drawing. Do you mean the first one? Yes, I got that and look at it every day. Little darling. It is nice that you are singing to her. I'd love to see that idyll. What a loss! I keep imagining it. Wasn't it nice to have some music again? A good selection of your music is safe! Tonight we'll play the gramophone with Beethoven concertos and the Unfinished, etc. – a bit primitive but still nice. I'll think of you a lot. Strength, little one! I have just been to the choir and shall take a bath now. Bye, love!

This is the only reference to Rie singing. Since she was a professional singer, it is strange that she did not continue with music in the camp, as did so many other women in the camps, deriving spiritual benefit from it. Quite likely she did not have enough energy left for that after the efforts to keep the two of them alive. She had an extra worry by now as the baby started to lose weight.

**December 1st [1943]**
Marijcke lost 80 grams this week. I had put her on five feeds, so that was probably the cause. I was very sad about it, but the doctor laughed at me and said I should not be worried. She has become much more mature

*Smuggled letter from 'Jeunesang'. The French was meant to confuse the enemy.*

this week, she laughs with a real laugh and talks a mile a minute when she is sitting on the potty. I feed her now every three hours and she sleeps through the night. Her little dresses really look sweet, she is like a real girl then.

**December 4th [1943]**
The feeding is not going well. Marijcke only gained 10 grams. Fortunately she is already roly-poly so I hope all will be all right again. She is so nice and sweet and lively, maybe this week will be a little better.

An additional disappointment was the fact that apparently some mail to the men's camp had been intercepted. "The drawing of Marijcke has not been passed on to pappie by those nasty Japs. It is such a pity. She looked adorable."

There is no mention of this in the next tightly folded slip of paper that arrived from the men's camp ('nr II, received Nr.1'). It was addressed to 'bébé Marijcke IV', from 'Jeunesang'. Apparently the use of the French translation of family names was meant to confuse the Japanese in case of an interception.

Henk could hardly write the letter for his hands were blistered from working with hoe and axe.

> One day I'll exchange *tjangkol* and axe again for pen and pencil, and as far as I am concerned it can be today, even though I am quite attached to the axe. It makes you feel that you still have muscles. It was a pleasure yesterday to fell a huge forest tree.
>
> That job arrived at the right time. I had just received your number 1 and no matter how happy I am to receive news (always after many days of impatient waiting), how happy I am with all the good news that is mentioned in it about you and our little Puck, feelings of sadness, regret and anger surface on such a day. When I consider the worries you have there, the hunger, the incident in which you are defenceless towards that burglar with our little girl there too, then it all becomes too much and I am quite desperate. You go crazy if you keep worrying on a day like that, especially because you cannot forgive, which would be the only solution. And then you can let yourself go in attacking such a stupid tree, even if it is only for an hour.

Another way to get rid of the negative feelings was to listen to music. Henk's neighbours in the camp had a gramophone and when he heard Rachmaninoff's piano concerto on an evening when he was down, he took his chair and joined the listeners and till bedtime found peace "in Mendelssohn, even in Liszt, because music takes you from the terrestrial to the divine. These are the moments in which you heave an intensely deep sigh, a feeling that I haven't lost even now, the next morning, the result of overwhelming emotions..."

Since Henk wrote this letter just before Rie's birthday, he enclosed a virtual big hug and hoped that it would be the last virtual kiss on their birthdays. The year before they had still been together in the Jozefschool, but his imprisonment (he called it 'the sordid affair') put an end to their family internment.

> The war, opinions or whatever do not concern me. I am only concerned with our small family. That is my task, the most beautiful one I can think of. It has been taken away from me...In any case, we'll be very close to one another on your birthday. Unfortunately we can only celebrate it in our hearts.

When Rie lamented: "Will that time ever return, sometimes I don't think so," he expressed understanding but then said: "This is not right. You'll find the confirmation in our small dear asset. She is for me the solution of all those questions that cannot be answered. Oh, how I miss what I have never seen."

He exhorted Rie (and himself) to be strong and spiritually courageous, to try to lift themselves from their 'profundis' with all their will and with the help of prayer.

> About your letter: wonderful that things are going so well with our little girl. When I read of little shoes, playpen (great that you got one), *pisang* and *djeroek* juice, then I realise how fast time goes and how I am missing a very special period (let's agree to do it over again once, for I do want to experience this too). Nice that she plays with her animals already. Does she like the rattle and the black dog?...
> 
> What a shame about the second drawing. Don't send any more, it is sad to lose them.

The embroidered coat of arms which he had intended to have framed was still lost but Henk did not think it stolen, probably just misplaced among the clothes in his trunk. He had not unfolded everything to search for it because of the limited space. "I'll definitely do it at the next 'airing' day."

> Well, I am continuing my writing. We just had a culinary lecture, something that makes your mouth water towards mealtimes. We have combined three anniversaries (Mr W.'s oldest son, Sm. and yours) into one, for which we shall try, with the well-known tricks, to manufacture something nice. The final decision was pancakes, and to this end I'll do my very best to produce something edible. I am also going to order some flowers from one of the gardens. That is all I can do. How nice that our little one is so cheerful. Does she give you, in spite of all the misery, also lots of joy every day?
> 
> Yes, when I think of the joy of the reunion and then for always, it overwhelms me at times. That should be something that makes all the preceding worry and sadness worthwhile. The two of us, crying with happiness, and Marijcke, crying with fear for a strange creature, a man!

With one of his friends, Henk started a quiz for the older boys. He found these quizzes quite difficult, because the boys in the camp seemed to lack pep, and were not open, honest and boisterous as he thought boys ought to be. Possibly the camp conditions made them indifferent and uninterested. With his usual positive attitude he remarked: "*Enfin*, we'll persevere and try to make something of it... I'll gradually get them in touch with all sorts of practical subjects, presented by people with practical experience. This is a unique opportunity for that."

Evidently the quiz did make an impression, because it is mentioned in a detailed description of camp life written by a secondary school teacher after the war:[21]

Once a week there was a question and answer session under the auspices of Mr. Jongbloed, during which the boys of the higher classes could ask questions for instance about future professions, or anything about social or religious matters. If there was a general interest in a certain subject, then an expert was found in the camp (and there were many of those in different areas) and invited to give a talk for the pupils.

One of Henk's camp mates, a young missionary, asked him to participate in a series of lectures about the life and work of St Paul. The lectures were to be followed up with personal talks, house visits. Henk was reluctant, and in his honesty to his wife admits to his own uncertainty. "I do not consider myself mature enough for this. There are so many questions every day that I don't know how to deal with."

The December letter ends with a final outpouring of affection:

Dearest, till next time, give the little one a firm kiss from me on your birthday and congratulate her with her dear mother, whom I love ever so much, far more than she'll ever know. All longing is for you both, let's keep courage and think of each other all the time. I'll also pray for you every day. Bye dearests, many kisses everywhere from your Henk.

## 10

# CANDLES FOR
# CHRISTMAS

Rie's birthday, 13 December 1943, marked the halfway point of the internment. The Dutch civilians had been behind the *kawat* for twenty months and another twenty months of ever-increasing hardships were ahead. Fortunately no one had any idea of that. It was the hope that liberation and freedom were just around the corner that kept them going. In her diary, Rie did not mention her lonely birthday, but described the improvement in the baby's condition. "This week our little girl gained 100 grams again. I am so glad it turned out all right. She now says 'grr, grr' and 'pfff'. She blows bubbles and gazes cross-eyed at her little hands."

A third letter arrived from the Sungei Sengkol camp, with the numbering showing that there were no gaps in the correspondence:

To bébé Marijcke. IV from Jeunesang
17/12 1943, nr III, rec'd nr II

My dear,
The mail has not closed yet, but I felt like writing already. First of all

another big post-anniversary and birthday kiss. To start at the beginning: on December 5th, which I have not mentioned yet in nr II, I thought of you a lot on the occasion of our wedding anniversary. I told Sm. the whole story of that day, including the *larongs*.

Henk's letter went on to describe the St Nicholas celebration – an important Dutch event. It is held on 5 December and centres around a bishop who comes by steamer from Spain, sitting on a white horse and with an entourage of black servants. Children who have been good during the year receive sweets and presents, while the naughty kids are beaten with a broom made of switches and put into burlap sacks to be taken back to Spain – at least, that is the story that everyone knows. The fun of the modern celebration is in the doggerel verse that accompanies the presents people give each other. In these St Nicholas poems, anything at all can be said about the recipient of the gift; it can be praise, criticism, ridicule, encouragement – anything at all.

In most camps, St Nicholas as well as Queen Wilhelmina's birthday were celebrated right up until the end of the war. Although by then the gifts consisted of nothing more than a handful of peanuts or a rice cookie, these celebrations were enormous morale boosters. It was important for the young children to stay in touch with Dutch traditions and served as a break in the monotony of everyday life.

In Sungei Sengkol, Henk wrote:

...the boy scouts had a campfire during which they put on a number of skits. Well done and fun. Then we all went to the recreation hall where St Nic made his entry and gave a suitable speech, in which many were given their 'sweets' and almost as many got the 'cane' (for stealing, etc.) And that was it.

The men in the camp were good to one another, creating special occasions and making an effort to surprise each other. Birthdays and anniversaries provided a good excuse for a celebration, as Henk described.

On Saturday it was Mr. Walr.'s birthday and we had the pancake party (of corn- and *oebi* flour). I still have the traces of it on my chest (six burns), caused by a few drops of oil during the flipping of the pancakes. But they were very good.

On Monday – your birthday – the men of my house surprised me early with a bunch of bright flowers that have been put near your picture. It was a very miserable day, rain and drizzle. In the afternoon the longed-for sun came out. With the help of two cans of corned beef I made a stew (hot water, thickened with *oebi*-flour, threw in some curry, then some finely chopped onions and then the meat that I boiled beforehand in the can). It was rather nice, served with mashed sweet potato and vegetables. In the evening we played the gramophone: Symphonic Variations (C. Franck), Beethoven's 3rd piano concerto (Max Hambourg), the 7th symphony (unfortunately very bad records) and the well-known suite for flute by Bach (in my mind's eye I saw Mok* tackle the main motif) the Brandenburg concerto and finally a polonaise by Chopin (personally I would have preferred the polonaise by Tip-Top, like last year).**

As you can see, a great evening with many guests on our piece of grass, while the moon rose in full unprecedented glory. It was the

---

* Mok was a well-known flautist who always stayed with Henk and Rie when he toured Indonesia. He was famous for the sentence: "This oratorium puts me in a sanatorium from where I'll end up in a crematorium".

** Tip-Top was Medan's ice-cream parlour, located in the main street; it's still going strong as a restaurant. During the internment in the St Jozefschool, Henk still had daily duties outside, and it was possible to obtain extra food and other articles. It is obvious from his comment that they had ordered the polonaise (ice-cream cake) to be delivered to the school during the December week of anniversaries.

moment for the Moonlight Sonata, which we did not have unfortunately. Afterwards I lay beneath the mosquito net thinking of you, as always.

Last night I had a wonderful dream about the three of us. I was walking with Marijcke on my arm. It was the image of what will be and, as we can assume, before too long. I woke up in a great mood this morning. She was so sweet. I miss her more than ever today. I am so very sorry that I am missing all those special times.

During the concert Henk was talking to the young missionary who had earlier asked him to participate in the choir and the bible studies. It turned out that this man had been in grade school with him in Zaandam, just north of Amsterdam. The missionary, whose name was Teutscher, was a few years younger, but his older brother had been in the same class as Henk. Through Teutscher, Henk discovered that his former classmate was then studying medicine and was under the wing of Carel Heringa, Henk's brother-in-law, and staying at his house.

Teutscher also knew all Henk's family in the Zaan, as the area around Zaandam was called. "As we talked I suddenly remembered two city boys who were received by us with contempt (pretty suit, curly hair, etc.) and jealousy (they came from the city!). They did not join us in our games (we wouldn't let them) on the mill or the rafts."

The partying must have been a little bit too much for Henk's stomach, by now used to bland food only. He developed diarrhoea and had to stay in the neighborhood of the 'tram', as the latrines were called. The doctor came around to assess whether special measures needed to be taken. Henk observed with wry humour:

What a job Verhoeff has to do every day, together with v.d.Steen (do you remember him, that Zaankanter whom we met in the school?)

Verh. talking: 'How are you doing? Hm! How many times today? Hm! Nothing yet tonight? Hm! A bit of sago today? Hm! Stay quiet and give a sample to the hospital today. Hm!'

And there goes Dickie again, to the next diarrhoea victim!

The next day Henk had to join the diet kitchen after all: "Must be my punishment for my joke about Verhoeff yesterday. My lunch now is a delicious plate of sago. It's like a slap in the face. I'll have to take it easy for a few days."

Sago comes from the pith of the sago palm. The taste of the sago porridge that later became the staple for almost all the camps was terrible. It was most often likened to the transparent white glue that was normally used for pasting wallpaper. All the prisoners generally loathed it and children often refused to eat it, even when it was the only food available.

The exchange of letters via the courier service of the Sipef employee was going well so that Henk and Rie kept up to date with each other's daily activities, problems and excitements.

> The day before yesterday I received your nr II with joy. You can deduce from the fact that I did not mention it right away that I do not attach much value to the rumours about transports. That is the general opinion here... Personally I do not think that they'll start such a massive move. There is no reason for it anyway. Don't let your attention be diverted from the food. It may be that the purpose is causing unrest. Let's leave it at that.
>
> You have not yet answered my question about how much oatmeal you still have. You started with 4 1/2 cans in the small chest. I have half a can. You gave some – unfortunately – to others.
>
> How much is left? And how much do you need per month as a minimum? I shall return that half can that I have. And I'll save some

more for you by exchanging stuff that I do not need anyway. You can count on one more can. How, I'll let you know later.

Henk was not as generous towards the have-nots as Rie seemed to be. He told her off more than once about giving food to people who through their own fault had nothing left. He had faith in God, but he was convinced that God only helped those who helped themselves.

Although the diary did not mention any St Nicholas celebration in the women's camp, Rie obviously reported on it, for Henk wrote:

How good that you also celebrated St Nicholas. It means that the old values still apply and that the spirit is high. Even Marijcke had presents. Great. She is already becoming quite a personality. From whom did she get that tendency for making fun? Surely not from the two of us!

Sunday morning – I am going to finish this letter now. The weather is miserable. The sky is completely covered and just now the rain started pouring down. Every time this happens I worry about your baby laundry. It must be very bad when things won't dry. *Enfin*, only a few days more and then the rainy season should be over. Everything is so wet and damp. That is probably also the cause of my diarrhoea. I didn't go to church because I want to stay near the 'tram'. In any case, the *obat* helped already and I have not had any more stomach pain – also thanks to the diet. Last night I only had to get up once. Brrr. Cold and dark and rain!

Many years after the war Henk talked about the hazards of having to visit the 'tram' at night. The latrines were open ditches that you had to straddle, standing or squatting. In the dark and wet everything was incredibly slippery and more than once people lost their footing and tumbled into the ditch. Unless it rained, getting clean again was a big problem.

*Christmas 1943 dinner menu. 'Woonwagen' is Dutch for gypsy wagon, 'smokkel' is smuggling, 'bedienden' is servants. Bandrek is Malay for a drink made of ginger, red sugar and water.*

Henk must have spent all Sunday morning writing for he went on about celebrating Christmas – "try to make it into something cosy if you can, also New Year's Eve" – and remembered the good times they had before the war: "the years that followed our wedding were cheerful, carefree years and we keep pleasant memories." Rie must have proposed to send another drawing of the baby, for he said: "Even though I would love to have a drawing, keep them safely and wait for a reliable opportunity. I'd rather see them later then lose them now."

By the way, they are trying to get a preacher to P.Br. for Christmas. If they are successful, what do you think about having Marijcke baptised? Personally I would like to wait until we are together again. What do you think?

Today I am having proper food again, for the examined sample turned out to be improved. Under your good care I never had any troubles like this.

With the improved health his humour returned – for he proposed to keep house together later, cooking meals together without servants: "Then we'll buy a coconut and a banana! Great!"

He ended the letter with the usual exhortations. "Grit your teeth, take care of both of you and keep the faith! All my love, your own Henk", and added as a postscript: "There is an excellent portrait painter here. He only charges two hundred after completion. What do you think? His colours (modern, bright) are excellent. If I could send it to you I would do it."

He did have the painting made – it shows a rather handsome young man with wavy blond hair and a rather stern look in his eyes. It stayed in the family into the next century...

CHRISTMAS WAS NEARING and in Poeloe Brayan gifts arrived – a rare occurrence.

**December 20th [1943]**
Today we received brown beans and dried fishes as a Christmas present from the prisoners of war. This fills our stomachs again. We were also allowed to send something to pappie. A second drawing of Marijcke has gone to him. Let's hope it arrives this time.

The baby was bothered by impetigo (pustules) on the back of her head. "She was crying a lot the last few days, but now they have opened and she is

*Portrait of Henk at the age of thirty in Sungei Sengkol.*

happy and lively again. I managed to get a stroller for her and now she rides in that every afternoon. She thinks it is great, kicks her legs with pleasure and says 'ah, ah' to everyone!"

On the same day Nr IV letter from the men's camp arrived:

My dearest darling,
Just now, when I returned from teaching, I received your nr. III. Great that everything is going well. The same goes for me. My diarrhoea is gone, I am getting proper food again fortunately. Before I use this hurried occasion to reply to your long letter, quickly the message that

you will get 3/4 (*septante-cinq*)* tin of oatmeal from Mrs. Pott, as soon as you receive this. He will write about this too. I'll try to do more for you, but with this amount you can last a while again.

I have written extensively yesterday and therefore I do not have special news right now. Unfortunately there is not much time for just banter. It would be so nice to be able to write without restriction in length about all that you think about. Today, for instance, I started a list on which I enter all the books, by subject (General, Art, Religion, Novel, History, Literature, Music, etc.) that I want to buy in due time in case our library, unfortunately, should have disappeared. I like that sort of job. Do write to me with some titles too now and then.

Henk had a strong trait of obsessive compulsiveness in his character. Making lists would help that tendency to organise life in times of chaos. The lists were among Henk's papers after his death; obviously nothing had ever been done with them. Most of the titles listed were never in the family library after the war.

He continued in his letter with some admonishing words – in her previous letter Rie must have been a bit too explicit about camp activities or Jap behaviour and if such a letter had been intercepted the consequences would have been dire. He pointed out that she had a great responsibility toward their little girl. Then he tackled a rather unexpected topic:

Sm. advised me about a small operation that would simplify the arrival of Marijcke's little brother and would make things easier. It is a small procedure, I can't understand why something like that was never noticed

---

* An old-fashioned form of *soixante-quinze* (the modern French for seventy-five) which is still used in Belgium and Switzerland. Henk worked for a Belgian company and obviously was familiar with this older construction.

or advised during the countless checkups in the past. I have tried to arrange for it here but the *obat* for local anaesthesia is almost finished and there could be more urgent cases. It boils down to an Old-Testament treatment. Understandez-vous?

Great that Mar. has gained so much. I am really glad – often worried about it – that it is still going so well with the feedings. Is she starting to sit up already? A playmate she'll get in x plus 9 months. Last time it worked exactly! I want to take part in this too, sometime. It would be fantastic to arrive in Holland with two kids.

I am glad that I bought that expensive rattle long ago. Good idea to save Jimmy for her first birthday. I hope to be able to give it to her myself. It must seem like a real zoo in her bed. Does she really cross her eyes, or just for fun?

The camps, bad as they were, were home to the detainees. They feared any move to another place for they were not usually changes for the better. Better the evil you knew, even with the drawbacks. "I would love to be alone for once, a small *tempat* of my own," wrote Henk. "Still, with our rooms of 4x3 and 2x2 we are well off compared to a *hong* of 60 to 70, one next to the other. But most of all I want to be with the three of us!..."

An actual move involved an immense effort for the weakened prisoners, as they wanted to keep most of their meagre belongings, often so necessary to survival, but they had to carry everything themselves.

Henk tried to allay the fear that Rie expressed and to give her something to look forward to.

The talked-about move is not accepted here. I also can't believe it. Don't let it spoil the Christmas days. Do you still have a candle to give Mar. an idea about Christmas? How I would like to hear her prattle away in the morning. That is going to be a nice cuddle party in bed in the mornings – especially on Sundays. Would she like that?...

Next time a more relaxed and longer letter. Many kisses and I'll be very close to you especially during the festive days. All my love to you both from your Henk.

**December 31st [1943]**
Christmas is over already – Marijcke's first Christmas in the camp and in the world. Very early in the morning, six thirty Nippon time, we heard people in the other camp sing 'Silent night, holy night' and 'Glory to God'. It sounded so beautiful. The rain poured down all day, the first day of Christmas. We had to celebrate it in our little *goedang* room, but Marijcke and I had a wonderful time together. In the evening I sang Christmas songs for her, in the light of the two candles that I still had. Peals of laughter greeted the candle flames and her big starry eyes shone with delight. I had decorated our little room with branches of fir and red ribbons – it looked very festive. There was no good Christmas food, nothing special at all, but in our heart it was a good Christmas.

This week 65 women and children were taken from the other camp because the boys had demolished the toilets for firewood. Even mothers of small babies were taken – the babies had to stay behind. The camp was going to be deprived of food for three days, but fortunately it was only one day.

This incident is described in greater detail in the diary of Truus van Eijk-van Velzen in the entry of 29 December.[23] She mentions that in Block E there were bathrooms which were unusable as there had never been any water there. Before long, the *atap* roof and wooden planks of these toilets had been stolen by young boys who made little tables of the planks for their mothers to sell and used the rest as firewood. In the end only the stone base remained.

When the Jap noticed this he became furious… They walked through the camp and noted down all the names of people where they saw planks. There were also ladies who had had planks for a long time already who therefore were innocent. But it was not possible to explain this to the Jap. In the afternoon the ladies and a few of the boys had to come to the office with some clothes and a blanket. There was quite a tumult. It was terrible to see. About 70 ladies were taken to prison. Mothers who had to leave 3, 4 and 5 children behind. These were taken care of immediately of course.

The whole camp was punished: no cooking or food tomorrow. So we started to cook right away for tomorrow. The kitchen handed out meat and vegetables with the rice right away, so we already had that. We won't be hungry.

## II

# 1944 – A BRAVE NEW YEAR

In the letters that Henk and Rie exchanged at the start of 1944, they were both hopeful that their imprisonment would soon be at an end. The fragmented information they received from the outside world, where the Japanese little by little were losing ground to advancing Allied forces, appears from their comments to have fuelled their optimism. Little did they know that it really would be different a year later, but not in the way they imagined.

New Year's Eve in Rie's villa was celebrated simply with a get-together and a potato and cucumber salad. "The whole house '*Welgelegen*' is celebrating it together… we hope the last one in captivity."

The men's camp had celebrated a more traditional New Year's Eve. No Dutchman will let that event go by without enjoying an *oliebol* – a kind of dumpling with raisins and currants, eaten with powdered sugar. The men in Henk's *koelie* hut must have thought up a camp recipe for it, for Henk wrote:

> In the morning I did the laundry, some household tasks, all sorts of preparations in order to be able to enjoy an imitation dumpling in the evening.

The celebrations for the whole camp included:

...a church service, very early. Not a good sermon. An old 'rev' from whom nothing can be expected, too bad, because it was a general service in the big hall... Around 9 the New Year's Eve celebration started in the hall. A short programme, rather nice. It started with a couple of negro spirituals, then a few NYE's stories by a pastor, then a part from the *Gijsbrecht*, followed by Thomasvaer en Pieternel.*

The content of the traditional message was very good. At the end the big choir sang two hymns. Back home I lit my three remaining candles and by this always romantic candle light we each ate three rice cakes that had become so tough that they provided us with a long time of pleasure. We legally recognised 12 o'clock NT (Nippon Time), and gave each other any good wishes we could think of. And then, because we wanted to eat something but had nothing to go with the camp coffee that was provided, we ate the morning porridge then and there! The strangest meal I ever ate on this special day. *Enfin*, the year starts off well and the chance that the next NYE's meal will be different is surely becoming a certainty.

My darling, a bright New Year's morning, that definitely looks promising. First of all a letter to you and – even if she cannot read it yet – to our little treasure who will, when you read it to her, answer with "grrr" and "pfff". Just that sound would be the most beautiful music in the world to my ears.

During my walk around the camp (that caused me a sore hand) they

---

* *The Gijsbrecht van Aemstel* is a play by the Dutch 'Shakespeare', Joost van de Vondel, which is traditionally performed around the end of the year, followed by a short comical opera about a wedding. The parents of the bridal couple, 'Thomasvaer en Pieternel', recite or sing a New Year's wish, which is still repeated in Dutch theatres every New Year. In Amsterdam, the sketch is adapted to parody local events and politics.

wished me countless times... "May you soon see your daughter." Really the strangest wish that I ever received.

Henk had not received an answer to his third letter and worried that it might be lost. His days were filled with physical labour, which he enjoyed, and reading. Besides reading light novels for relaxation (he even called them 'decadent') he also concentrated on his spiritual edification by studying the confessions of St Augustin, which he saw as "a kind of counterpart to the '*Imitatio Christi*', but in the Protestant sense. Extraordinarily beautiful! Man with all his desires, all his senses and lust, in his battle against God. For me it is even more realistic than Thomas à Kempis, although the thoughts of this 'hermit on the mountain' are often more subtle."

His state of mind is reflected in the following paragraph:

In my own words I wrote on a piece of paper:
> Hours, days, months, years
> Of rough violence and the misery of war
> Please keep us for one another, Lord
> That is our prayer tonight.

And with that prayer I thought in the first place of my own family (especially since that word has acquired a much deeper meaning now), but also more generally, for slowly but surely this is no longer a 'wish' but in many cases a dire necessity. And then it is a comfort that God knows about this necessity, even better than we do. He is the beginning of all things, but also the end, and it is my heartfelt desire that we'll experience that soon. I can only hope for a miracle. Sometimes I wish that the solution of this bloody tragedy will not come with the thundering might of weapons, a human victory, if we can call it that, but in a revelation of the living God, in such a way that we as people would be able to recognise it and that it would therefore have a post-war spiritual blossoming as a result.

He wrote another long poem that emanated from a heart bursting with questions, asking God for another miracle, to bring delivery, the end of the war, to give them strength to live according to His will. The present time he called "purifying years". Later, both Henk and Rie declared that these years in internment were very important to them. They even said sometimes that they would not have wanted to miss them – a statement that was shocking to hear.

This sentiment was far from their minds on that first day of January 1944 when Henk recorded the New Year's day meal:

It was a great rice-table that we just had – '5 courses'. If it could stay like that... but I doubt it. However, we manage to get what we need. The best thing is not to dwell on it. If towards mealtimes you are just sitting there waiting for it and talking about it (as so many here do) then your hunger pangs are much greater, than if you just keep reading or do something manual.

Sweetheart, I am almost at the end of my allotted length. I am happy that I could write to you on this New Year's Day, and even happier that this is sent right away. Let's hope that the year '44 will be a real *Annus Domini*. Until then we pray separately from, but no less for each other. Keep courage, little one. The confirmation of that in your letters gives me strength in this present life. All my love and many kisses for our little girl, for whom I long intensely, as much as for you, is that all right? Many kisses and lots of love, your own Henk.

Rie remarked on the glorious start to 1944 and wondered in her diary entry of 2 January whether the "beautiful weather" is a good sign. "Could it be that we are together again soon?" She had had to put the baby on extra bottle feeds to try and build her weight back up. The baby hated the afternoon feed but, wrote Rie, "it seems to be good for her, she is a bit more cheerful. She was really becoming rather quiet lately. Normally she can be a real clown, bats her eyelids, hisses like a small cat and then bursts out laughing."

She also recorded that the women taken away a week earlier were not back yet. The other camp was being deprived of fruit for a month as punishment.

Cards arrived at the camp from husbands and fathers who had been taken to Burma to work on the railway there. They brought both joy and grief, for at times they reported the deaths of men who had succumbed to the terrible conditions.

Eight days later, Rie was relieved that the supplementary feeding had worked. Her baby had gained 140 grams and was more cheerful and playful. "I am very glad for I was really worried." The weather was starting to get her down too. "As gloriously as the new year started, now every day is gloomy. Rain every day and then more rain, the whole camp is a mud pool, it feels as if you are going to drown in mud."

Anyone who knows the tropics – especially rural areas – will known exactly what she meant. Incessant rain turns paths into muddy streams. Soil sticks to shoes, thickening the soles to grotesque platforms on which it is impossible to walk. Sandals or flipflops throw mud on the wearer's head and back. Going barefoot is the answer. Fortunately the rain is usually warm and so is the mud – feeling it ooze between the toes is not an altogether unpleasant sensation.* However, cleaning up after being out in the mud was a luxury that the women in the camp did not have.

Her despair was deepened by what she saw happening around her. "The

---

* I learned this first-hand many years later when I worked as a doctor in a village in Java where there were no paved roads and access to most houses was via narrow tracks. When I had to go on house calls during a downpour, I soon learned to go barefoot.

women have still not come back from prison, and this week another three were taken away," she wrote.

> The situation is getting more and more hopeless, almost no food any more, treachery abounds, the weather is depressing, there is no news. At times it is very, very difficult to still keep the faith. The contact with Henk is also so much more difficult. When will the end come? Will we ever leave this wretched Sumatra alive? Sometimes I doubt it.

Rie was never as optimistic and positive as her husband. In later life she often suffered from depressed states that fortunately never developed into the real depressions. Fortunately here in the camp she had to keep going to keep her baby alive and in turn; she was enjoying the antics of the baby that gave her the courage to struggle on.

> Marijcke grows, unaware of all the misery around her. She blows bubbles, reaches with her hand towards anything colourful. She tries to sit up all the time, and with a little help she is quite successful. When you look into her cradle you forget a lot of the camp misery...
> Today she was in the playpen for the first time. She thinks it is wonderful, to be able to move hands and feet freely. She got a bit excited because the whole kindergarten class was gathered around the playpen carrying their little chairs on their heads.
> We received a 'Christmas' package from pappie, with lots of soap*, a can of jelly and little fishes, what a treat! We were so happy. Maybe pappie will now also receive the package with the drawing of Marijcke.

---

\* When as an adult I worked abroad, parcels from home always contained lots of bars of soap. It was amusing: didn't they realise it was easy to get soap where I was? Maybe that urge to send soap was a throwback to camp times.

**January 29th (1944)**

Marijcke is now 5 months old. This week she gained 170 gr. She is starting to become really nice and fat and has round apple cheeks.

She is in the playpen all day now. She has already managed to roll from her back onto her tummy. She was radiant with joy. She is a real joker. A few days ago she was in her stroller and suddenly she sat up straight laughing out loud with fun. All the other children started to laugh too and she almost couldn't stop any more. She is already indicating when she has to go on the potty. Then she starts to cry and groan. When I react by putting her on the potty a broad smile appears on her face.

Just how important the letters were to morale was underlined when the system of smuggling them broke down, as it did from time to time. "It was a shame to hear that yesterday the pail with letters, all of them, ended up in the hands of our friends. An unforgivable mistake," wrote Henk on 30 January when he composed a replacement for the one that was lost.

The breakdown in communication was very upsetting. Henk wanted to share his inner emotions with Rie and spent much time on each letter. He was deeply disappointed when he found out that his letter had not been sent and then was intercepted.

There is really no contact in the full sense of the word. They are just signs of life. Reading that both of us are healthy and keep courage, etc., that is the most important thing, and with that we should be happy. At times it makes me depressed.

Depression was not a word in Henk's vocabulary, normally. He always seemed in balance, although at times his inner feelings surfaced in his poetry.

Later in life he learned to control himself even better, and often people thought that he was a severe, heartless person. Those who knew him well recognised his hidden characteristics – his ability to sympathise with people, his compassion for those less fortunate than he and the sense of humour that helped him cope with every situation he encountered. And when times were tough he used to quote the motto of the Dutch engineers who built railways across Sumatra through incredibly difficult terrain of mountains and jungles: *Moeilijk kan ook* – 'Tough is also possible'. But at this point he was just thirty years old and impatient:

> Just to think that you are only a fifteen minute drive away from here with our little girl that I don't even know yet, although she was five months old the day before yesterday and the last news I had from you was written on Christmas day, over a month ago. That is really miserable. You can take a walk in the sun, you can sit and read a book, you can enjoy the flowers, etc. etc. and yet, what good does it do? The days go by, in fact they fly past, because I immerse myself in a rush of physical and mental work, and yet... all the days are lost. I think I am complaining like Job. I rarely do that and yet it has to come out some time. This afternoon it has really hit me.
>
> In any case, I notice in your letters that you have these 'ups' and 'downs' too. Who doesn't? What did we do wrong that we have to live like this, now already for almost two years? Oh, to pray every day in the correct way, how difficult that is.

Then he pulled himself together again, remembering that one day the war and the internment would be over and that the life afterwards would be worth all the effort and the grief. "And God will give us strength." He described the work he had been doing that week – outside the camp in the five hectare sweet potato plantation. "You are free then of all duties except chopping wood. Five days a week outside from 9 – 12 Nippon time. Hoe, pitch, clean. Wonderful. You forget all the limitation of freedom and you feel great in the morning sun."

Unfortunately this outside work was stopped because some people abused the relative freedom. They could still go out to chop and saw wood and haul it to the kitchen. "Thus I have already been in the forest this morning to cut down trees, great morning exercise. Next to me a guy with a cocked gun, as if there is anywhere I could flee to!"

Even though it was relatively easy to get out of the camps, the Western detainees could not flee because they could not hide anywhere. Their size and skin colour were just too conspicuous and they would need a lot of help from outside local friends, who would be risking their lives.

The birthday of Dutch Crown Princess Beatrix on 31 January provided an opportunity for a welcome break in routine.

> In her honour we organised a sports day for the boys with nice prizes. A relay race, long jump, tug of war, baseball, afterwards a communal lunch outside (*nasi koening*), then 'who or what is that?', then a costumed football match and in the evening camp fire with a story (by our v. Balen), songs, tombola, dinner. And that is the end of January, fortunately.
>
> This week I was out one afternoon in a deserted *oebi* plantation, about half an hour walking away from here, to cut sticks and take them to our plantation. Such a trip is fantastic. I obviously got too much sun that day, for I still have a fever blister on my lip. You wouldn't want to kiss me!
>
> Outside we also dug up *oebi* roots for ourselves, with eight of us. I gave away my portion to Teutscher and other thin guys. A little bit I fried for myself. Wonderful...

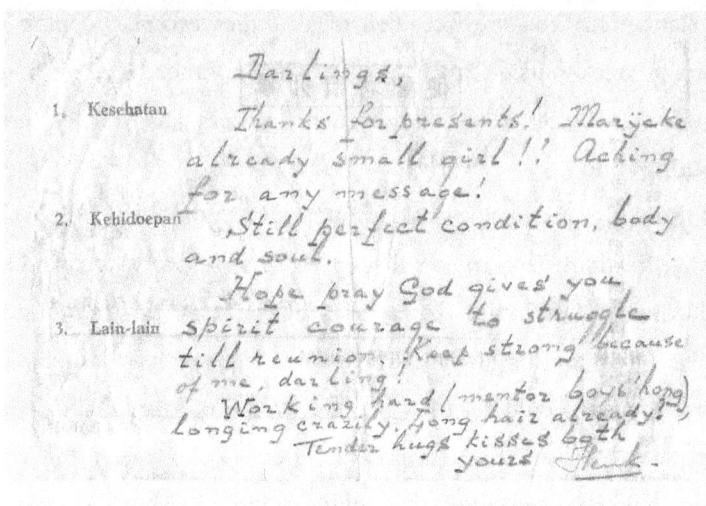

*Red Cross note from Henk.*

Henk finally found the embroidered coat of arms, hidden in the pocket of a pair of pyjamas that he had not used yet. He had it framed and cherished it then and throughout the years. Also, he reported that the Christmas parcels had arrived and brought great joy to all the recipients in the camp.

> Many thanks for the colourful book cover. We shall admire it together next Christmas. I immediately put it to good use. The little calendar is nice too, with beautiful fine Rie-stitching. The black silk at the back had of course been taken apart. Something special might be hidden there! My joy was rather diminished when I discovered that the picture of our little darling had been removed. That's the second now that is lost. We heard that all pictures, drawings, portraits etc. were torn up. I won't report the words I uttered. We understand each other. Such a darn shame, for I was longing so much for that. Please do not send drawings any more. Just keep them, for they take the place of photographs. I'd rather see later what she was like than nothing at all.

Henk had many questions, mostly about the baby: Were the feeds going well? Did she like her stroller? Did she lie in her play pen in the sun now? He reflected that "the most dangerous time is now in the past, luckily. In four weeks time that little thing will be half a year old already. That sounds really special."

He wanted to know if his Christmas parcel had arrived and whether there was anything Rie needed urgently. He thought it was "sensible" that Rie had bartered a pair of shoes. "Very important. I never walk without and therefore I have no ulcers." He told her he was trying to collect another can of oats for her. "Very difficult at the moment. But it'll get better…"

Here the optimist spoke again. The facts painted quite a different picture: many people were sick, there was influenza in the camp, probably due to the change in the weather, and anxiety reigned because of the rumours of a transport.

> Well, my dear, it is late. I have to take the pots to the kitchen again for the daily *oebi-rampat* hotchpotch. Brrr. I often call that drall-balls or *oebigant* because of the terrible perfume taste. Tonight is the last night of my week of house duties.

Henk quoted a Dutch poem by van Rijnsdorp that he called "a jewel". In spite of the shortage of space on the paper and the shortage of time in which to write letters, he continued mentioning poetry and religion. It was obvious that he derived his strength from this.

> My dearest, stay strong. I will make you forget all the misery as soon as God brings us together again. Together we will then, remaining together, build our future, the three of us (for the time being)! Who knows how close this is already. Keep going, kiss our little darling from me and for

you all my love, and many long, fond kisses from your own Henk. I love you very much and think of you all the time.

January ran into February and in Poeloe Brayan, the baby reached another milestone: her first tooth. "She is a bit fractious but it really isn't bad. She is a brave little girl," Rie wrote on 3 February. "Yesterday I took her visiting and she sat laughing so loudly that all the people sitting around her had to join in."

In his next letter (nr VIII) Henk was not aware of this event for it was an answer to Rie's letter (Nr V) written three weeks earlier: "There was great joy when a sign of life arrived yesterday," he wrote in a letter dated 8 February. "It had been so long since we had heard anything. You would like to have a letter every day, but unfortunately that is not possible. I was very glad to hear that both of you are healthy and that you are keeping courage. That's the way it should be."

The only way Rie and Henk could keep courage was to believe that the end of their misery was close at hand.

The darkest hour is before the dawn. That the hours are already dark, we both know. We are in God's hands and that is my daily comfort for there we are safe. Your belief in this I have read with joy.

He was convinced that they had a future together in which they would be united in their attitude towards life and their belief in God. Others too found strength in faith. Henk was impressed by the 'home service' that his friend Teutscher had made for himself, which covered the whole year. It was "not a diary with thoughts, but indications of texts and a short liturgy. Extraordinarily nice. I am going to copy all of it so that we can have this for us both later."

Some people were copying recipes by this time but for others it was religion that played a big role in life. Although Henk did not mention it, the various religious groups in the camp kept to themselves, holding separate services and often keeping alive the differences that existed between them before the war. In the last year of the internment, a schism split the two Christian Reformed groups. They could not settle their different approaches, which even existed in something as trivial as the rhythm to which hymns were sung. Curiously, at the same time, back in Holland, there was also a schism between the same two groups although for different reasons.

Henk appears to have adopted a pragmatic approach. "I have learned to appreciate the liturgical service here. In church we already sing whole and half notes (the Christian Reformed brothers are opposed of course) – sounds much better."

He still did not know whether his Christmas parcels had arrived and, speculating that Rie would have "wondered about the careless mix of articles" that he sent, is keen to explain what had happened.

> We knew nothing about the possibility of sending parcels, until on the first day of Christmas they suddenly said: delivery within one hour. I was on vegetable duty and by the time I could stop with that for a bit, I only had 10 minutes. They did say that there would be another opportunity the next day but I did not trust that (a good instinct for all the parcels of the next day were refused). In 10 minutes I just grabbed everything that could be at all valuable for you. I still considered sending 1 blanket, 1 tin of butter (my last) and a sheet, but I did not dare do it. By making 2 parcels I tried to spread the risk.

He listed the articles – cans of food, bandages, soap, thread, pain killers and disinfectant. He regretted later that he did not send the butter when he heard that Rie's stock had run out.

I am still sorry that the second drawing [of Marijcke] is also gone. The clandestine way is after all still the safest, for all your letters are complete. The numbering is very practical. Oh, in my parcel there was also a Blue Band tin with roasted peanuts. They probably got stale, although they went into the tin red-hot, as they were just standing on the fire as a Christmas treat.

He also noted that both camps were apparently getting the same rations, but possibly he did not know that young children only got half rations. Even so, it was never enough. "It is unfortunately imperative to cook something extra. Even though it arrives via crooked roads, they are also God's roads.... We also hardly ever see any fruit, maybe one *pisang* a week. What's worse is that you and especially the children are not getting it."

Henk did what he could from a distance. "I almost have another tin of oats for you," he wrote. "Do you know someone there who would give something like that to you so that I can give it to the husband here? I'll ask around too."

Rumours of transports kept surfacing. In fact, there was truth in them. The tide of war was gradually turning and the Japanese were getting worried about maintaining their iron grip on the detainees when the Allies reached the Indonesian archipelago, which they now feared would not be long in coming. There were plans to gather all the internees into central areas, away from the coast, so that they could be controlled more easily. Henk saw a positive side to this:

There are still vague indications that there is a plan to put everyone together on one plantation. If that would mean that we'd be together again, so that I could help you with everything and could have our little Puck with us, then I'd be OK with that. But as far as we know, nothing is ready and that says a lot. Also, I can imagine that you don't fancy uprooting, especially now with the extra stuff needed for Marijcke.

Unfortunately, the camps that were created later that year were not meant to house families. Again, Henk and Rie ended up in camps that were only at a few kilometres distance from each other, but with even less contact than what had been possible in Medan.

Henk described his vicarious enjoyment of his daughter's development.

By the way, whatever you write about that little darling is wonderful for me to read. Especially delightful is the story that the tip of her tongue appears whenever she is planning something naughty. Oh, how I'd like to see that. I am so glad that she provides you with so much joy amidst so much misery.

Nice that she is starting to discover the many possibilities of the rattle. Did you tell her that I bought it? Does she like the play pen? I bet she sorts the toys by preference in '*lakoe*' and 'not-*lakoe*' and then after a few hours falls asleep in the midst of the mess.

I really want to experience all this also, at home. I hope that you will be physically fit enough later that we can start with it right away. But if we have to wait 6 months or so, then that is also quite possible. Maybe even better, because there will be plenty of novelties.

In the event, they did not manage six months. They were re-united in September 1945 but had to stay in the camps for another month or so, due to the insecurity of the situation in Indonesia at the time. Their son was born in September 1946, just a year after their reunion.

It is hard to imagine what Rie must have felt like. Certainly she would have needed closeness and affection, but it must have been very difficult to be pregnant right away when there had not been any chance yet for her body to recover.

Henk's letter continued with bits of poetry by Johannes Reddengius that he was reading, obviously trying to share the benefit he found in the words:

> Accept the bread that you must eat in solitude.
> the drink that's bitter on your tongue.
> When the pitch darkness of suffering descends,
> then have courage and walk with steady feet,
> searching for the stars that burn brightly in the night.

Henk told Rie he had pasted the drawing of his daughter into his pocket bible "together with two pictures of you. The third one has been framed and hangs near the painting in my corner."

After several days in which the men had been forbidden to work outside on the plantations, they were allowed to go out again – much to Henk's relief. He preferred to be busy so that there would be less time to think.

> We did indeed go outside again this morning after about 14 days of rest. There is lots of weeding to do. I weeded for 2 1/2 hours among the beans, etc. Good back exercise. Burning sun overhead, wonderful free view and 'the good earth' under your feet.
>
> The morning goes fast. Although you work harder, you think less about food, you don't feel like smoking and you are nicely tired when you get home. Then a dip in the *pantjoeran* (self constructed 'waterworks' in the shape of a dammed up stream with flow pipes), then dinner and now I am lying prone to write....
>
> I've had it pretty quiet for the last three or four days. Gone to bed early because I did not feel like talking. We are running out of topics. Then you suddenly get irritated with all that senseless chatter. We have a special talk

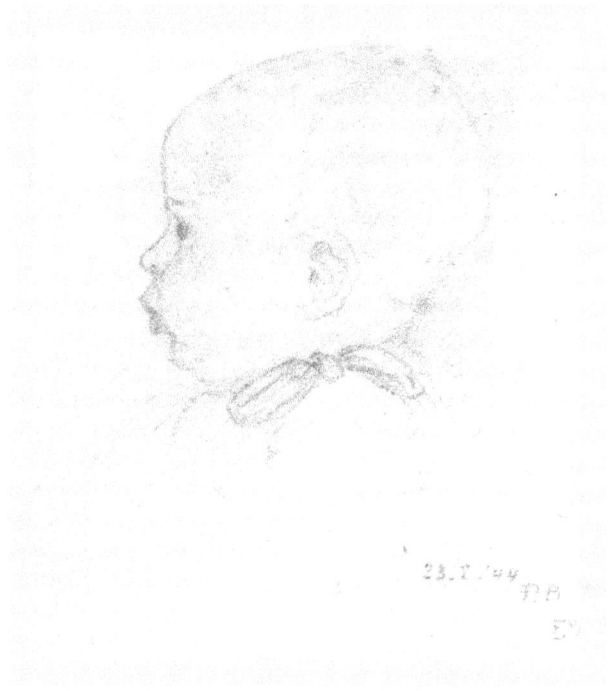

*Baby Marijcke, Poeloe Brayan, 23 February 1944.*

group, always talking and never doing anything. Still we have a rather good *kongsi*. Never dubious talk, no bad language, no quarrels.

Well my dear, time for dinner, the usual hotchpotch is on its way. Can we please never eat *oebi* again after this?...

You say 'It would take a miracle and they don't happen any more these days.' I don't agree with that last bit. Maybe less visible than once upon a time, but there are still definitely events that we can count as such. Marijcke? My arrival here? And I am strongly convinced that we'll see more this year. We can also hope that the end will be a real *'Deus ex machina'*, so that no one will blow his own trumpet and boast about his own strength. That would also have so much influence on the future.*

* Did the atomic bomb count as a *Deus ex machina*?

He hoped that Rie still found the time to write the baby book and encouraged her to "write especially about the funny things, just like you pass on in the letters now and then. I love it when you write in detail about that." Like the doting father, he wanted to know if his daughter was good looking and smart for her age.

For his part, he told his wife he had been writing poetry fragments again, and would share them with her in his next letter. "Everything that occurs to me with reference to books, conversations, impressions, I always write down right away."

Writing poetry obviously was Henk's way of letting off steam. Some of his fragments were not very 'Christian' minded':

> *Ik haat hen met volkomen haat,*
> *Ik wens hun lijken in de straat.*
> I hate them with perfect hatred,
> I wish to see their bodies in the street.

> *Ik weet het zijn uw scheps'len wel*
> *Met hun gele zwavelvel*
> *Linea recta uit de hel.*
> I know they are supposed to be Your creatures,
> They with their sulphur skin
> straight from hell.

With impatience he cried:

> *O kom toch met uw wonder*
> *Duizend dagen dit gedonder...*
> Oh, please come with your miracle!
> A thousand days of this misery...

## 12

# THE LAST LETTERS

For quite a while no more letters arrived from the men's camp. It is possible that there was verbal communication via fellow internees who met their spouses in the doctor's or dentist's clinics. These opportunities were always used to relay as many messages as possible, but there is no record of this. Rie continued her diary, meant to give Henk an idea how his family coped in the camp:

**February 13th [1944]**
From pappie we got the news this week that the portrait of Marijcke has been torn up by the Japanese. Poor pappie, now he still doesn't know what his baby looks like. When will he be able to see her?

It is getting more and more difficult in the camp. We now are forced to work one hour per week on the land and to make rope for two hours, three days in a row. We are already so tired!

Marijcke already eats *nasi tim* from the central kitchen and she loves it. Unfortunately she still has many sores – a real camp ailment.

Her second tooth can already be seen.

**February 24th [1944]**
Marijcke's second tooth has broken through. She has already been eating rice porridge from the kitchen for a week. That made her gain 270 grams this week.

**February 28th [1944]**
Today our little girl is half a year old. She celebrated this day by refusing to lie down in her stroller. Now she is looking around sitting up properly and she laughs out loud to anyone who passes. It is such a sweet little woman with a very strong will. When she eats *nasi tim*, I have to shove it into her mouth between two of her fingers. Of course that makes a terrible mess. I wanted to wean her off that habit, took her hand in my hand and held it tightly, however much she struggled and wriggled. Then she thought of something else. A strong sneeze with a mouth full of *nasi tim* and mammie, together with the wall of the room, was covered. Then she yawned excessively, choked and coughed, which sprayed another dose of *nasi tim* over mammie. Then I forsook all parental wisdom and shoved the *tim* into her mouth again between her little fingers, and the naughty girl was laughing!

The baby seemed to develop normally in spite of the lack of vitamins and variety. She rolled onto her tummy now, and crawled throughout the play pen, attracting people's attention and interacting with them with funny noises.

What was not noticeable at this time was that the lack of Vitamin A due to the poor diet was stopping the normal development of her night vision, resulting in severe night blindness. She had no such problem in daylight and recognised familiar things, including Henk's portrait. On 18 March, Rie recorded that her baby "reached for it with both hands and with a radiant smile she said: 'pa-pa'! Every evening before going to bed, she looks at papa's portrait and into the mirror. Sometimes, when she is very tired, she tries to hit the portrait and her mirror image but when she is sweetly sleepy, she laughs and crows and says 'papa'!"

Rie had another drawing of the baby done, but she "was so restive and curious that it did not come out too well." Her impetigo had cleared and Rie observed that "she has a perfectly nice little head."

The baby was starting to be quite a handful to control, demolishing her cradle by strong kicking and falling off the dressing table:

> I had nursed her and wanted to put a clean diaper in her cradle when I suddenly heard a dull thud and there lay Marijcke on the floor, face down. Fortunately the mosquito netting had broken her fall, so that she did not hurt herself. She did not cry at all.
>
> When she sits in her stroller, she pulls all sorts of funny faces at the people she meets. She squeezes one eye tightly shut and with the other she watches if people find it funny. When she sees them laughing, she joins in, laughing loudly. She is a real little clown, always ready for a joke. In the bath she does not lie back as sweetly and quietly as before but she kicks so much that everything gets wet.

Around mid-March, the management of the camp changed. The camps of Java and Sumatra, which were considered to be in front-line areas, now came into military hands. The detainees did not realize that this was actually a good sign – a sign that the Japanese were getting worried about the outcome of the war. All that mattered to them was that the new commander made changes, some for the better but inevitably some for the worse too. From 1 April the milkman was cancelled. Rie "decided not to worry about it. God will take care of us." She reasoned that "up till now everything has gone so well. Would God then desert us towards the end? I do not believe that for a minute."

On 9 April, she wrote in her diary that "the new Japs arrived and with them we also got more food, fortunately." Lists of new rations were put up in the camps: Per adult per day – 250 grams rice, 150 grams corn, 20 grams salt, 20 grams sugar, 5 grams pepper, 1.5 grams tea, 200 grams vegetables, 50 grams meat (if available), 20 grams oil. Children were to receive half rations, and extra milk, almost 1.5 litres of milk per day, was allocated for sick people.

It did not last long.

Marijcke was allowed to keep her milk, gets better *nasi tim*, but unfortunately no fruit. We now get three meals: rice porridge in the morning, at midday rice, vegetables and a piece of fish. In the evening corn, those nice hard kernels, but at least it fills the stomach. I am not walking around with hunger pangs.

Against all the odds, Rie wrote, her baby was growing and developing into "a wonderful headstrong thing and extremely witty". The "little lady" no longer wanted to lie down while eating or going out. "Eating while sitting up causes tremendous messes, but she has to learn. What's difficult is dressing or undressing her while she is sitting up."

Bad things happened all the time, but when a baby died, Rie was particularly concerned.

In the other camp a tragic event took place today. One of the women who was taken to prison had a baby of a year and a half, a completely healthy child when she was taken away. Yesterday the child suddenly had a fit. After much discussion with the Jap the mother was finally allowed to come. During the night the child died, it was buried this morning at eleven thirty and at twelve o'clock those Japs came to take her back to prison. And all that because she had a potted plant in her room.

At the same time that the coffin for the child was brought they delivered a large coffin for the next case. The deaths are now starting, four in one month. Our resistance is diminishing and it is only your will to live that keeps you going.

What a joy it is to look at that radiant Marijcke and what a fearful possession. Only God can save us for one another.

Rie did not mention that Easter had arrived – it was obviously not celebrated in any way in the women's camp. That same weekend Henk wrote a letter that commemorates an important event:

(on the outside: to bébé Marijcke IV, from Jeunesang SS)
Nr. 10 Easter Sunday 10/4 (1944). Received nrs 8 and 9.

My dearest darling,
Easter is almost over. Historical days for us. We got engaged seven years ago. We were not together at that time either. We really have spent many special days and birthdays away from one another. When this is over, that should never happen again.

I did not have any duties these days, so it felt a little bit like a festive holiday.

Like so many of his letters, this one too listed the activities he did to keep from worrying – do the cleaning and the laundry, attend church services, chop wood, prepare lessons and take a First Aid course. "There is a lot of variation and the variety is just what you need most."

He was always happy when letters arrived from Rie, he said, "especially when it appears that – God be thanked – you are still doing all right under the circumstances." A drawing of his daughter had finally arrived, by unofficial post. "I am over the moon with it," he wrote. "The clandestine way is really the safest. Now I have something at last. Oh, how I'd love to see our little girl for real. Everything remains so unreal this way."

Henk had lost his *kongsi* friend, the surgeon Smook, who had been sent to work in a hospital again. For Henk it was "a real pity. I'm getting used to it, but the first few days it was really quiet."

The way Henk wrote about this friend in his letters gave the impression that they were very close. In the NSIO diaries, a long piece written by Dr Smook after the war described the hut that they shared:

> We lived very quietly and hardly ever went to the gate. Our little hut was in the periphery, close to the *kawat*. We enjoyed the *pantjoeran* that had been constructed in the little stream and I worked with dedication outside the camp on the fields in order to make our camp self-supporting. We had to cut down rubber trees and clear the undergrowth.

Smook mentioned many of his fellow internees (like the two men who played bridge incessantly and the black man from Surinam whom everyone called Snowwhite), but strangely enough never referred to Henk who was certainly one of the 'we' that worked on the fields.

Henk tried to make up for the loss of companionship by creating a special area for himself.

> I have now moved my bed to the corner. In as far as a corner in a *koelie* hut can be cosy, I really have a cosy corner now. When I lie on my bed in the afternoon after work and look into the gardens on my left, with on my right everything close at hand (books, a cup of tea, a pipe or self-made cigarette) then I love to think about you, about our future, in which I have more and more confidence.

The situation here has not changed much since the first of April. Less *oebi*, more rice/corn, in total 275 grams a day. With a few extra vegetables it is just manageable. It leaves you with a healthy appetite the whole day, all the time. Still, I feel really great and if it is not going to get worse, you'll see me again, unchanged, just a little bit older with some traces of time. But who does not have those and we all wear them with honour.

Again he expressed his longing to see his daughter, to be able to provide her everything that is needed for normal growth. He referred to her naughty behaviour as a sign that she was all right.

Henk's concerns for the health of his wife and daughter found an outlet in 'business matters', as he put it: the food bartering by proxy that went on in the camps.

Did you get the large tin of butter already from Mrs v.d.W.? From that I could not give Drijvers* a pound, but I had just received a tin of 1 pound from Sm., so I gave that to Dr. If you returned that pound to Gini [Drijvers] already, you can now ask it back. Please confirm the receipt of the butter. If not, then ask Mrs. v.d. Werf.

It is striking that these transactions were done in good faith – and if they succeeded most of the time, it sheds a positive light on the character of the people involved. To give away a pound of butter – or oats, in a similar arrangement – under those circumstances, trusting that someone you didn't know would return it to your loved one, must be incredibly difficult.

Henk asked Rie to confirm that the deals went through without a problem.

---

* This barter was also mentioned in Drijvers' diary in the entry for 11 April 1944: 'From Jongbloed I received 3 x 10m thread as well as a pound tin of butter, so that worked out just fine'.[21] Thread was a code for money; in this case thirty guilders.

"Above all I hope that the large tin of butter arrived." He deflected her concern that he was depriving himself of anything. "Don't worry about my *barang*. I have and keep more than I need. We don't have to worry about 'afterwards'. Do you now have the opportunity and the means to cook something extra?"

> We had a pepper distribution here! I have enough for the next three years and that is only 1/4 of what we are getting this month! There is always something to laugh about, if things weren't so sad. With the *obat* this week we got enough laxatives to keep all of us going for a year!

Though a surplus of pepper and laxatives was something to laugh about, the daily ration of food usually wasn't. Instead of meat all they got was one small fish the size of a small sardine per day each. Henk hated fish with a vengeance. "Just the thing for me," he wrote. As it was their only source of protein, he ate it "bravely but not with head and fins like many here do."

The previous week they had enjoyed the first harvests from their camp gardens outside the *kawat*. Much of the produce had been eaten by the wild pigs. "Still it was a nice result of our hard labour."

On 11 April, he wrote that he would not be able to enjoy his newly made space for much longer.

> The two vacant places in our house are going to be filled tomorrow by Blom and his son.... Everyone, especially those from the large *hongs*, would like to come here. That son of Blom, however, is ill and needs a lot of help, for him it is quieter here. So tomorrow it'll be a mess again here.

Koop Blom was a teenager and kept a diary throughout the camp years. It is included in the NSIO diaries. Although he was regularly incapacitated by his illness, which may have been an auto-immune disease, he managed to keep chickens, study for school, do handicrafts to make presents for people and make drawings that showed real talent. He survived the camp but died prematurely due to the damage his body had incurred in nearly four years of internment.

That spring, however, Henk's thoughts were for his wife's health. "You lost a lot of weight, my girl! Be careful, please." For her height and build, he thought sixty-eight kilos was a minimum. "There is not much we can do about it, but still you have to watch out for yourself…"

As usual, pride in his daughter's achievements were tempered by the frustration of not being able to witness them.

Is Marijcke such a brat? What a milestone that she has already said 'papa'. I am as proud as can be. And how are the attempts at sitting without support? I hope so fervently that I can be there for 'the first step'. She is going far too fast, tell her that. Is Molentje satisfied with her growth and progress? She has already doubled her weight. How did you solve the milk problem? I hear that your camp has received goats. Are they for the milk production? That's OK, but you have to add a lot of water.

Henk commented that he was "glad to hear that you can still occupy yourself with piano and singing," and encouraged her to "keep at it." Surprisingly Rie mentioned nothing about this in the baby book, and in later life she never referred to making music in the camp, even after watching the film *Paradise Road*, a story based on fact about a group of female detainees who organised a voice orchestra to lift morale. Apart from the singing at Christmas, references to music-making are absent from the diaries of other women as well.

In the text of a lecture written in 1977, Rie did mention that she gave small concerts on a piano that happened to be at Aek Pamienke, the last camp she was in. How a piano got there, out in the jungle, is one of the idiosyncrasies of war. She also mentioned that she carried music scores with her all that time.

Henk concluded his letter with more words of encouragement.

> Little one, I have to stop again, unfortunately. Till next time! Kisses for the little girl and yourself, all my love, Henk.
> We have to be stubborn and persist a while longer, thinking about each other a lot. We are being taken care of, we know that. Bye.

Shortly after this letter was written, a poster issued by the commander of the internment camps was published in the camps with the following text:

> It is strictly forbidden to buy or sell goods from an internee. Any requests should be made known in the usual way via the camp leaders. People should get used to small inconveniences in a war area.

Since most people had not yet lost their sense of humour, the term 'small inconveniences' from then on was used ironically in all the camps.

A 'small inconvenience' of a different kind was experienced by Rie and recounted in her diary. The entry was dated 14 April 1944, which she noted was the second anniversary of their internment: "Two years away from home and family."

> Last night I hit a Jap. I had lit my lamp because a rat was rummaging around in the room. As usual my window was open, but fortunately my pails with laundry were standing in front of the door. I was just getting back into bed when I heard someone knocking on the door. I called: 'Who is it?' No answer, but the knocking continued. I went to my window,

opened it a bit more and saw a male figure pushing against the door. I asked what he wanted. 'Ssst!' he said. He tried to open the door via the window and then suddenly grabbed my shoulder. I hit him on his hands as hard as I could, so that he let go, and then I saw it was a Jap. It frightened me, because you are not allowed to hit these gentlemen.

I called my neighbour who came out of her room. The Jap turned towards her with outstretched arms, holding his high boots in one hand. She yelled loudly, at which the camp leader came running – and then he wanted to embrace her! We went to get the guard, who came running with his revolver in his hand, but by that time the culprit had disappeared.*

As for the baby, fortunately she slept through it all, Rie wrote, going on to describe her daughter's development into "a very independent young lady... She wants to sit by herself on her potty, does not want to drink from a spoon any more but from a cup, and does not want to be dressed lying down but sitting up."

Rie found it necessary at times to discipline the headstrong girl but she did not take that without protest.

Earlier this week she hit mammie. She was sitting on her potty, suddenly decided she did not want to do that any longer, and stood up in my lap with stiffly stretched legs, I tried to press down on her tummy, but that made her so cross that she hit me hard in my face with her strong little hands.

Time and again there are small domestic problems, recorded for Henk.

* Many years later Rie described another 'rat incident' in greater detail: "One night a big rat tried to get into the cradle of my baby and I hunted for him, armed with a big piece of wood. He tried to escape through a hole in the door, but he lost his balance and fell into a bucket full of water. I always put the bucket behind the door, so that no Japanese could enter my room at night time. This wet bath terrified the rat so much that he never returned and we had a good rest at night from then on."

Individually mundane, together they are the annotated score of a young life: new teeth, more falls, small acts of sabotage by the baby. "She is getting so wild and lively," wrote Rie on 28 April, "that at times I don't have enough hands."

> Today she tore the mosquito netting completely off her playpen and lay wrapped in tulle like a little bride. Of course, she thought it was great fun. Now she is sitting, ramrod straight, in her playpen hammering everything with her bone teething ring. She now sings all the time; maybe she'll be a singer too.

This must have been music to Henk's ears. In early May, he noted with fatherly pride that she was "cosy and naughty and cheerful." He thanked God that both Rie and their daughter were healthy and that "our little girl is growing up so well in spite of all the shortages," particularly fruit. "Oh, when will I have the two of you with me again forever? You have no idea how intensely I long for you and how much I think of you. Practically all the time."

He complained that he had to write his letter of 5 May in a hurry and regretted that he had not started a letter earlier, because he was doing some repair work to his clothes. Later in life he never was an enthusiastic do-it-yourself man. Sewing tears and attaching buttons would take him a long time.

Rie must have sent him birthday wishes for 8 May, because he thanked her although clearly he was not looking forward to the occasion: "Three days to go. Get it over with quickly," he wrote.

He expressed concern at Rie's weight loss and advised her to give up gardening. This was quite unrealistic because the extra vegetables were a dire necessity. His wish "to have a healthy Rietje back" seems rather selfish.

In the men's camp as well, the food was "not exactly luxurious. In the morning 50 gr of porridge, in the afternoons and evening 90 gr, a total of

*Henk was a compulsive writer of lists, in this case of calories.*

230 gr. Sometimes a bit of *oebi* rubbish. But plenty of vegetables from our own gardens."

What they couldn't grow, they tried to acquire by barter, but even that was getting difficult. "Incredible what you had to give in exchange for some sugar," wrote Henk, adding ominously: "Almost nothing to be had, I understand. Here there is also a lot of bartering. Also high prices for everything."

The shortage of specific food items was not limited to the camps. When Henk wrote 'nothing to be had', he was referring to the fact that by then, the local population in Medan and throughout Sumatra was also suffering hunger. There was a complete breakdown of infrastructure in the islands. The plantations had bad harvests, and there were no imports of anything at all.

Many of the local men had been taken away for forced labour elsewhere on the island, even abroad, and fields lay fallow.

Sometimes the inter-camp barter system let them down, as appears to have happened about the time of Henk's letter. "The butter from v.d. Werf left here really almost immediately after my first report," he wrote. "I fear the worst. I really hope you'll still get it. A large tin would mean a lot to you. *Enfin*, I have tried my best..."

Losing a large tin of butter would have been a catastrophe that would depress any other person. Henk's reaction was absolutely typical. He was self-assured, did whatever he had to do as best he could and never worried about the outcome. He was never beset by doubt – his best was good enough. He completely accepted that there was nothing else to be done.

Of the missing butter, he wrote: "I would never have eaten it myself anyway." He asked Rie to have them look for it seriously once more, then turned to the subject of oatmeal. "Do you need more? If so, tell me, then I'll try again. I still have a lot of stuff to barter with. I would be very disappointed if you did not get that tin. I had been so happy when there was an opportunity."

Reading was still Henk's way of keeping his mind off the worries about food and health. Like many Dutch, he read equally easily in his mother tongue, English, German and French as is reflected in the lists of books that he drew up from time to time.

> I read *My life as Carola*, a rather strange book. Many good thoughts, still weird. You didn't like it, right? Then also a French book, very humoristic, about Japan. I am also reading *Eyeless in Gaza* by Aldous Huxley. Very difficult, some of those sentences. Still a book to keep. I'll never want for reading matter here. There is so much good stuff around. In between I also read *Jews without money*. Very good. And many poems.

My darling, only a few more words, then it is dark. The sky is beautiful. I am sitting here so comfortably but so alone, in spite of the 670 men. How wonderful it will be to catch up with the backlog of love, happiness and cosiness in the peace of home later. May God give that that time comes soon. I am very confident about our future. I long so much to spoil you again with all sorts of things, especially the non-material. That too, but above all I want to show you how much I have gained in my heart through this time, and I know that the expression of that will be dearer to you than presents. A life in true harmony. Till now we have always been winners, and in this time, especially through our little girl, doubly so! Many kisses for both of you and much, much love from your Henk.

Rie was to receive no more letters from Henk during their internment, although it seems unlikely there was no more communication between them until the end of the war. Any news that trickled through was by word of mouth, but none is recorded in the baby book which Rie continued to write.

Around the same time, an extraordinary document came into Henk's possession and remained among his papers. Typed in English, it may have been issued sometime in 1943 or 1944, when the various Arakan offensives (in northern Burma) took place. The only Indian territories where the Japanese ruled at that time were the Andaman and Nicobar islands.

The Colonel Kurokawa's farewell speech to Dutch subjects
1. I have now been ordered by the Nippon High Command to join the Chief staff of the Nippon Overseas Forces in India.
2. It is only about a month's time since we have been working together but yet it seems to me to have been a long period of as much as ten years.

3. It is with the deepest regret that I am not to address to you words of farewell. Leave-taking has always been and will be the object of poetry and tragedy everywhere through all generations, and for all of us the day will draw near when it will be inevitable to say good-bye.

4. Yet, however, our 'good-bye' does not mean to say good-bye to our work. No, to the contrary. We are striving at the same aim, to establish peace and in this lies our big task. Nobody would like to hear the sound of a canon again, and so it is my earnest hope to create eternal peace. Carried by this hope in my heart it will be possible for me to start with confidence.

5. To make Sumatra the most important of the New Asia is my deepest, honest desire in my life, as it is obvious to me that this achievement means happiness to the human beings and helping them to accomplish their endeavour for everlasting peace, and which of us is not longing for this. And for this reason I always meant to talk to you with boldness. There must of course, now, be a parting but this is meant to be a physical one whereas in accordance with my honest thinking, we still must remain in contact in our minds.

6. Finally I do wish that you and your families will always enjoy good health, the most essential factor to be enabled to work hand in hand with full energy. With pride, hope and cheerfulness I am looking forward to having carried our big plans for the erecting of a new Sumatra.

Good-bye to you!

## 13

# MORE ALONE THAN EVER

**May 5th [1944]**

The fourth tooth, upper front tooth, has arrived. It was a difficult time for our little girl. She protested a lot.

We do not have any light any more, are no longer allowed to cook ourselves, so that we have to run back and forth with our pans and stand in line to get something warm. Life has become less cosy for Marijcke because now I have no time at all to spend with her. But the news from Europe is good.

Rie didn't elaborate, nor of course mention how the news from Europe arrived. It could have been via a hidden radio, possibly in the men's camp, or the Indonesian-language newspaper may have had some information about the latest developments on the fronts. The parallel diary of Truus van Eijk[23] mentioned a cease-fire in Europe and a US ultimatum to the Japanese, but dismissed them as just rumours, which they were...

The conditions were taking their toll on her health and that of her baby. Writing on 17 May, she commented that her little girl "was not well for the first time" the previous week. "She cried one whole night and had a temperature of 38C at night." Fortunately, by the time she wrote her diary entry, the baby was back to normal, "lying next to me in her cot practicing 'papa, mama and me' while taking everything apart, her diaper and sheets, so that she is lying partly on her bare mattress."

For herself, Rie recorded being "really ill with jaundice", unable to eat for a week, with "a beautiful yellow complexion so that I look like a wasted war victim."

Did she not see herself as a war victim until then? She was close to desperation – as were many of her fellow-detainees. Truus van Eijk mentioned that the situation was now unbearable. It rained continually, no one had shoes any more, there was no wood to burn to cook food or boil water for tea, and most people had neither money nor stores. The nurses advised people to stay in bed as much as possible in order to save energy and lessen their hunger pangs.

> It seems as if the world around us is asleep, as if we will still have to spend years and years here. It is beyond sad. When will God deliver us from this?

**May 20th [1944]**
Marijcke is no longer a cradle baby. The cradle was becoming too small and hot for her. Today I rearranged my whole room and put the playpen inside, and she sleeps in there now. It is nice and spacious for her and she sleeps well in it.

This week had many emotions. First the rumour, 'the incoming mail has been seized.' Fortunately it was not the mail that had been seized, but the man. He was beaten up severely and we had no food for one evening. But the camp directors provided food after all, because they managed quickly and quietly to have something cooked for us.

Three deaths in one day, amongst which two young women, one a mother of 6 children. Even the Jap got scared and recalled the spoiled fish. We no longer get an evening meal, no sauce, no more fish. Menu of the day: rice boiled in water in the morning, rice and some vegetables in the afternoon.

Again mail from Sengkol seized. Nine women had written via a private mail. They have to go to the other camp, are being questioned there, and beaten up.

Suddenly there was a raid to look for electrical appliances. Not much success. They did find a roll of *gula djawa* and one packet of cigarettes, for which the responsible woman was given 15 days of *tjangkol* duty.

The next day the main Sengkol mail was seized. This time we were all involved. The whole day we were tense about what was going to happen. In the evening we were interrogated, our letters were read with lots of imagination by Mrs van Genderen. We got a long lecture and the worst punishment is: 15 days *tjangkol* duty, from 10 a.m. till 2 p.m. and 4 p.m. till 7 p.m. Many women have already fainted. I am not being punished because of my jaundice.

One of the NSIO diaries[21] added detail to Rie's description. It commented that there had been sixty-five letters from Poelau Brayan which Mrs van Genderen was forced to translate into Malay while the women of the camp stood listening. "She did a great job," wrote the diarist. "Every one of the letters was the same: one long story about the lack of food etc. The *hantjo* was unable to control it. Of course we were chuckling inside about it." But as time wore on, they stopped laughing, and at the end of three hours, many had fainted.

Rie wrote that the camp was still being interrogated when a "new smuggling affair" was uncovered. "Today they took away one sack of our rice."

It was food they could ill afford to lose. Rie's weight had dropped by four kilos in one week, leaving her feeling "hopelessly weak and miserable". The baby was struggling with the heat and her teeth and was "very fractious. This afternoon I was very cross with her when she knocked a mug of milk out of my hands. She howled at the top of her voice."

### June 14th [1944]

Finally some courage to write again. I've been so hopelessly down all that time. Jaundice renders you weak and listless for so long.*

Marijcke and I both had a bad 'flu. Coughing and completely stuffed up. Difficult days and nights. She grew another tooth today. She was such a cry-baby the last few days, she wanted me to be with her all the time, something that is very difficult in the camp.

In general she is a sweetie. She has discovered new toys. An old toothbrush and a mug are her favourites, she plays with them all day.

She had a very bad tummy, at one time 7 dirty nappies in one night. There was no light, another punishment. It was a terrible hassle to have to do everything in the dark.

With a new commander who was "like a devil" there were daily upheavals in the camp. House searches always brought something forbidden to light and punishments were the order of the day. Reading and handicrafts were forbidden and the women were no longer allowed to drink tea or play bridge together.

> ...we feel really harassed. This week two women were beaten terribly,
> 45 minutes, with belts in their faces. Their eyes and faces were bleeding
> heavily. Yesterday evening we heard that Camps A and E have to move to

---

* Almost thirty years later I had first-hand experience of this, having contracted hepatitis A during a vacation in Indonesia. My liver was damaged so much that even months after the initial high fever I was still so weak that I needed two hands to pour milk from a bottle. That my mother was able to take care of herself and a baby while suffering from this disease is amazing.

Gloegoer, the former prisoners-of-war camp, so we think that the soldiers there have left. Mrs van Genderen, our camp leader, and the doctor will have to go too. A great loss for our camp.

**June 18th [1944]**
Marijcke is not doing well. She now is getting a whole row of teeth and suffers a lot of tummy aches. She gets colds all the time, either a dripping nose or a cough. Mammie consequently does not get much sleep, for there are dirty nappies all the time, at times six per night. She lost a lot of weight, one pound in two weeks. She looks a bit thin, but it becomes her. She now has such a very finely chiselled face.

She is also getting a bit too naughty, she is a real spitfire. If she really does not want something, or is a bit too tired, she throws herself backwards, hits the ground with her head and beats around with her hands. But she's still my little girl. When she is in a good mood, she is so sweet.

Mammie cannot pay enough attention to her. Life is so busy with work and duties and then Marijcke just lies there, crying.

The move of some of the women to Gloegoer took place and in Poeloe Brayan 'tante Zus' became the camp leader. One immediate effect was a quietness in the camp. "We are not upset all the time by all sorts of rows," wrote Rie. "Also a bit better food, fortunately." She was horrified by the treatment meted out on a friend. "It was terrible. The Japs beat *tante* Loet till she was half dead. There were seven men beating her in her face and on her back with belts."

Even worse from her personal point of view, "there are no more letters from pappie." It was a good thing Rie did not know at the time that she would receive no more letters until the month of the liberation. Ahead of her still lay thirteen months with practically no news and with forever worsening conditions.

"Another new month and still no freedom in sight," she wrote on 9 July. Her heart went out to the 1,050 women and children who had left for Gloegoer that week. "It was sad to see all those careworn women in rags trudge by. They had to carry heavy loads on a half-hour-long trek. The lovely commander walked behind with a whip."

A few weeks of teething and colds affected the baby badly. She lost almost one kilogram of weight in one month.

> I have now opened my last tin of butter for her and so I put a little bit into her daily *nasi tim*. That does a lot of good. It made her gain 180 grams in one week
>
> Last night she gave me a real kiss on my cheek, when she had to go potty. She really likes cosy cuddles. She lies back against me with her eyes closed, humming softly. Her toys now consist of a large mug with all sorts of little pots, stick and tins. That keeps her busy most of the time. Her dolls and animals are carelessly shoved aside.
>
> This morning again a baby in the other camp died. Now all the babies that were born around the same time as Marijcke have gone. It is so terribly sad and I pray to God every day that I may be able to bring my little girl through this all without problems.

In the other camp Truus[23] mentioned that she ate slugs for the first time. "It made me puke, but that was really a matter of the mind, for they did not taste bad at all. The doctor approves, because snails and slugs contain a lot of protein and fat." She recorded that a cat had also been consumed, adding: "If we don't get more food soon, we won't last another three months."

The slugs "were hard like rubber, totally unpalatable," another ex-detainee recalled. "I used to rub them over my upper arm where my sweat had left some salt to make them taste a little better."

Another survival trick was to force yourself to eat slowly, and in this the children of the camps proved adept, as some recounted sixty years later.[29] "We invented all sorts of ways to make the food last longer, such as eating with teaspoons. Then we discovered we could stretch the meal even longer if we ate with the other end of the teaspoon. Rice we ate grain by grain, of course."

For Rie's daughter, the situation added a new dimension to her baby instincts. "This week she stole a piece of dried rice from me," Rie wrote on 23 July.

> Someone presented it to me, her eyes went wide and suddenly she
> grabbed it and it disappeared into her mouth. She almost choked on it,
> but that did not stop her. She eats everything, rice cakes with *pisang*, corn
> cakes, she loves it all.

Fortunately, the camp was getting a bit more food again after "difficult days" with lots of work, standing in the sun for hours on end. Rie wrote that appearing at roll call wearing a housecoat would earn the detainee the punishment of additional *tjangkol*, etc. Then she added: "From 1 September we won't get vegetables and firewood any more. It is getting more difficult the closer we get to freedom. When will that be?"

Her baby's first outdoor bath provided some diversion from the hardships of the camp.

> I put the bath in the garden and at noon she played in it, surrounded by
> a large crowd of admirers. A rubber turtle was allowed to swim too and
> she had lots of fun. Full of mischief she hit the water with her hands,
> and shook the edges of her bath so that the water went over the side.

She looks very well again, glows with health and vitality. Her hair is starting to grow now. She is getting a nice blond crest on her head, with even a small curl in it.

**August 5th [1944]**
Marijcke is looking good again and she is becoming quite naughty. During the air-raid alarm exercises she practised sitting without support, now she is trying to stand up, which is difficult for her because she is so fat. She gets very cross then and sits there in her playpen with a bright red anger-face, hitting her knees with both her hands. Countless times she falls over with her potty, sometime she lies where she rolled under the bed together with her potty and contents. She does not sleep much any more during the daytime, so my siesta is out the window too. She is really quite an enterprising kid, and she takes no nonsense from the other children. Her bath in the garden is still a high point of the day.

The air-raid exercises had been going on since the beginning of May, together with regular black-outs. While the knowledge that Allied aircraft were getting close enough to worry their captors must have helped the women's morale, the exercises themselves, especially the black-outs, caused problems. For Rie, it meant she had to take care of the baby or prepare extra food in the pitch dark.

Rie observed and enjoyed more milestones in the baby's development, undoubtedly wishing that Henk could have been there to witness them too.

**August 16th [1944]**
Marijcke was taking a ride around the camp in her stroller. Suddenly she saw the goats and she stood up straight in her stroller. She crowed with pleasure that she finally did it.

She is becoming so witty, our little girl. Last week she sat playing in her playpen with a small bottle and the stay from a corset. With her small fat hands she stuffed the stay into the bottle, stirred around and then smeared imaginary ointment between her toes, exactly as she sees happening in the clinic every week. In her bath she throws water over her head with a powder tin and snorts like an adult in the shower. She performs a very funny: 'put your hands together, dei, dei, deï'. The funniest bit is where she has to hit her 'bad' head with both her fat little hands.

**August 25th [1944]**

Marijcke is standing. She pulls herself up on the rim of the playpen and stands there tottering on her fat legs. I now have to tie her down in her stroller, otherwise she'll tip out. You have to put away everything out of reach of her small grasping fingers, for everything can be used as toys.

Fortunately we got *pisang* again. Ten days we had no fruit, because the men in the Belawan camp had sent mail and we did not give the letters to the Jap right away. We've had a difficult time again and everyone has lost quite a bit of weight. Only Marijcke has gained again.

In three days she will have her first birthday. Pappie won't be able to give her his doggie himself. When will he be able to see her at last, our little sunny darling?

**August 26th [1944]**

Marijcke stood up without support! I just left for a moment to heat up her *nasi tim* when she suddenly became very angry and stood up, crying loudly and peeing in her pants. Later she did it another few times but now she sits again and stays put.

There was no date for her next entry but it had to be 28 August 1944: "One Year!"

Marijcke's first birthday!
She woke up at 6 a.m. in the best of moods. I had put the toy dog from pappie on her dressing table. With sleepy eyes she looked at it, a big smile appeared and she shouted ecstatically: 'ta, ta, tit, tit, tat!' I told her that she had gotten the dog from pappie. With radiant eyes she looked at pappie's portrait and with eyes full of love at the doggie.

I tried to put her back into bed, but she was so excited that she could not get back to sleep. Quickly I put her playpen outside and set up a table for the presents – toy dog and dress on the table and pappie's portrait next to it. Then the neighbours came with presents. Marijcke shouted with joy, kept calling 'aaah!' which means 'hurrah!' and waved with her hands above her head.

Rie wrote down the whole list of presents complete with the names of the generous donors. Besides the black furry toy dog from Henk and a dress from Rie, her toddler was overwhelmed with presents: toy animals, bibs and dresses, socks and clothes hangers, a silver fork and napkin ring, as well as flowers, material for dresses and wooden dolls.

The birthday did not start so well, because the camp was being punished once again and we were not allowed to cook, not even to heat up the porridge for the babies. Fortunately I had been given an egg, Marijcke's first egg. I beat that through her porridge so that she had something special after all.

That may have been the intention but wasn't the result. Much later, Rie

*Jimmy the first birthday dog. It survived intact until 1991 when the author's first puppy got hold of it and tore out the wood shavings stuffing.*

recalled that the first time she had got hold of an egg, she had soft-boiled it, but her daughter refused to eat it. When she mixed it in her porridge, again the baby refused to eat. Finally she gave up and ate the porridge and the egg herself.

Rie had made a cornflour pudding the day before, but "it had collapsed. With corn and *pisang* I had made nice cakes that the children loved." The children enjoyed their treat and sang the traditional birthday songs, the baby joining in "with a hoarse voice while banging her head with her spoon".

> She was in a fun mood the whole day. During her bath in the garden she sat splashing and kicking, laughing loudly. She was so excited that of course she could not sleep that evening, due to all that emotion. I had to take her into my bed at night, where she was still making fun and shouting 'hurrah!' until she finally fell asleep, tired out, with her head on my chest.

So that was our little one's first birthday. How very differently we had imagined it. Now we can only hope that pappie will be there when she becomes two years old.

In the men's camp, Henk received a rather pastoral letter from Rev Henk Teutscher* on the occasion of his daughter's first birthday, and it remained among the camp documents that Henk kept.

He that dwells in the secret place of the Most High shall abide under the shadow of the Almighty. (Psalm 91:1)

    A life that was desired for many years and that was born in days in which a human life hardly mattered any more; a life threatened by danger, disease, hatred and enmity as if it were prey; a life, for which a mother's heart sacrificed whatever it could still sacrifice of its beggarliness; a life that brought pain to the tortured love of a father's heart; a life in the midst of roughness and monstrosity, where the love of parents is unable to provide beauty, purity and tenderness, a young life that has been carried through all this until this day, is that not a miracle of God?

    Such a miracle is your Marijcke! Thank God for it on this day, entrust her safely in the secret place of the Most High and teach her later to abide there!

    My warm congratulations, God bless you!

    Henk 28/8/1944

---

* Although my father had not kept in touch with Teutscher after the war, contact was renewed almost by accident twenty years later when he read a 'help needed' ad in a mission magazine. The Teutschers were looking for a foster family for their youngest daughter, Paula, for they planned to return to Indonesia as missionaries. A few years later I shared student digs in Utrecht with Paula's sister Liesbeth for five years while we both studied medicine. Liesbeth, her mother and her brother were also held in the jungle camp at Aek Pamienke during the last months of the war.

After the excitement of the birthday, Rie reached the lowest point of her life in the camp.

**Sunday September 3rd [1944]**
This is the darkest day of the internment. The whole day rain, rain, hunger and hard work. We have to clean the whole camp. Hours of *tjangkol* duty and lugging grass. Food for the baby has been reduced so that I give a part of my food, which is not too much already, to Marijcke. I am weak with hunger and misery. I don't have any shoes any more. I trudge through the mud on bare feet, with open ulcers under my feet.

Oh, life is unbearable. It is as if God has totally deserted us, as if we have drowned in this pool of mud.

Fortunately Marijcke is cheerful, but very tiring. Sometimes I am unreasonably cross with her, because I almost can't manage any more and I am so tired of all the worries. We do not have light in the evenings, so that everything has to be done in the dark. A hopeless hassle with a baby.

**Sunday September 10th [1944]**
Marijcke gained another 260 grams this week. In spite of getting less to eat, she keeps prospering. This month of September has been very gloomy so far. Pouring rain every day. As soon as you put one step outside your *goedang* room, the mud reaches over your ankles. We don't have any shoes any more, my wooden sandals have partly disintegrated so that I always touch the earth with my toes. The result is that I have rotting ulcers on my feet and legs. On my calf there is a huge carbuncle, hellish pains!

The humidity in the tropics touches all textiles and leather with mould. The white fungus eats through the materials, making them crumble easily. Most of the time the women in the camp wore wooden *tekleks*, but they still needed a leather or rubber band across the instep, and these became a weak point.

There was still no light in the evening, so the only time the women were not "toiling and moiling", they were sitting in the dark. Rie's baby had become a toddler and a talker, walking all around her playpen and talking a mile a minute – "all gibberish". She was intelligent, noticed everything "and then copies it like a little monkey," wrote Rie. If she got hold of a pair of manicure scissors, she would sit cleaning the nails of her toes. With a comb and hair brush, she brushed her little round head. "She is such a sweet darling and fortunately she has no idea of the misery all around her."

> The camp is becoming worse and worse. The work increases, *tjangkol* duty, cleaning cesspits, cleaning ditches, carrying wood, lugging heavy rice bags... and the Jap gentlemen stand there grinning. Even all the sick people had to *tjangkol* for two hours at the hottest time of the day. Yesterday a doctor of the medical staff was here, and then no one was allowed to *tjangkol*, because the doctor should not see that.

It is quite possible that the senior officers of the Japanese command never had a precise idea what was going on in the camps. They were regularly inspected, but that caused upheaval in the camps for the women had to work extra hard to make the place spic and span for the visit of the VIPs. These inspections never resulted in any improvement of the conditions or the treatment of the detainees.

> On Sunday I wanted to spend a real Sunday with Marijcke. I got up early to do all the work and was ready by ten o'clock. Then all of a sudden I had

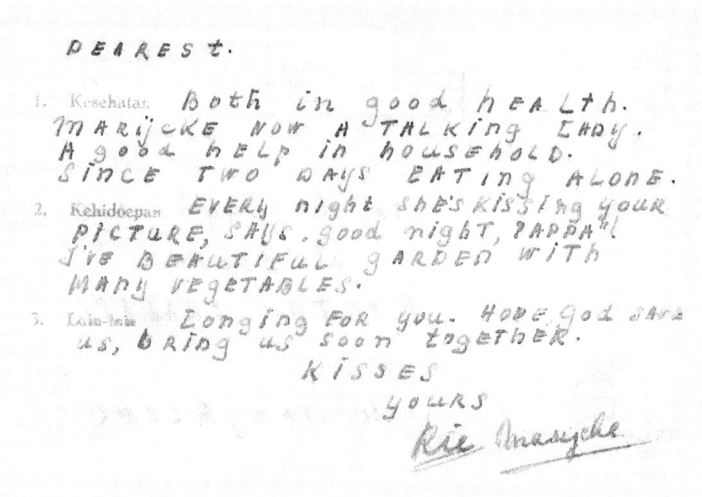

*Undated Red Cross note from Rie to Henk.*

to carry wood and vegetables, four hundred coconuts, bananas, clean the *kaki lima*, and at three o'clock the whole camp was required to clean the ditches till 8 o'clock. My ulcers became much worse because of all the dirt. The doctor had to cut them yesterday and now I have to have bed rest.

That bed rest was relative. Because she had no help, Rie still had to clean and do other jobs from seven to eleven-thirty every morning. Then she could rest until dinner time, but if she wanted a coffee or anything else, she had to get up again. Her daughter meanwhile was cutting more teeth, this time another molar. "It did not bother her very much," wrote Rie. "She just sucks her fingers all the time and drools all over the place."

### October 2nd [1944]

There are rumours that the men have left the camps and that we also have to move. No one knows where to.

This was no rumour. The men of the camps around Medan were being moved, first a few hundred, then thousands. At some point the women would have found out where their men were, but it probably took months for the news to be confirmed. The uncertainty was almost worse than anything, for in the past some moves had meant transport overseas with all the dangers that they entailed.

## ꔷꔷꔷ 14 ꔷꔷꔷ

# DEATH CAMP

In October 1944, the men and boys of Sungei Sengkol were transported to a new camp, Si Rengo Rengo, that had been established inland, in an area of rubber plantations and jungle. Two hundred 'strong' men were picked out from among prisoners of Sungei Sengkol and one other camp and ordered to prepare a camp in the same area for the women and children who were to go there later. The women's camp was called Aek Pamienke. Henk counted himself among the 'strong' but there is no record whether he was part of that particular work detail. From the diaries of some who were, it appears that these men were able to hide notes and messages for the women in the buildings that they erected. Henk and Rie never mentioned any of this.

Neither did Henk mention the transport to the 'valley of death', as the camp in Si Rengo Rengo was called. It must have been quite terrible. First they had to walk eight kilometres to the Sengol station, laden with all their belongings, which included as much of the produce from their kitchen gardens as they could carry, as well as their chickens. Then the men suffered a two-day train ride in slatted cattle cars, from which the dung had to be removed before they could sit down on the bare floor, forty men to a wagon.

*Impression of the train trip to 'Death Valley', a drawing by teenager Koop Blom. It conveys the mysterious and threatening atmosphere of the journey to the camp at Si Rengo Rengo.*[21]

Although the detainees were angry at being put on display like cattle in these cars, closed cars would have been much worse in the tropical heat.

They stayed overnight at Kisaran station, where the sleeping accommodation was the stone floor of the platform or the stinking planks of the wagons, with millions of mosquitoes making sleep next to impossible. An open ditch dug along the side of the rails served as a latrine. Meals for the second day were provided by the local hospital, which was run by the Swiss.

Then, after they arrived at Rantau Prapat, the end station, there was a six kilometre walk to the river Bila. A ferry that was dragged back and forth on a rope stretched across the river provided the only means of crossing to the camp. The river had to provide their drinking water, bathing facilities and sewage removal – but first the drainage of the open latrines had to be rerouted, because the camp builders had located them upstream from the *pantjoeran*, the wash place. The Bila turned out to be in spate much of the time and then bathing was impossible. Even at the best of times, prisoners had to be careful as there were crocodiles around. At the slightest infringement of camp rules, the gates to the river were locked and the men were unable to get water for drinking, washing and cooking, sometimes for several days on end.

The *hongs* of Si Rengo Rengo had been thrown together carelessly with *bilik* walls and *atap* roofs. None of it was particularly waterproof, certainly not in tropical downpours. Each *hong* had four sections of bamboo platforms in two storeys. The lower floor was fifty centimetres above the ground. The distance between the two floors was about one and a half metres, not enough for a European of average height to stand erect. The living space allocated to each person on the wooden platforms was seventy-five centimetres by two and a half metres. Suitcases and chests had to be stowed at one end, and mattresses rolled up in the daytime to provide some sitting space. There was no room for anything else, so the men had to spend all their time in these cramped conditions, 220 men in each *hong*. On the endless gloomy wet days of the rainy season, this must have felt like a cold version of hell. The buildings were so rickety that in a strong wind they swayed. After a few months, several had to be shored up because they were in imminent danger of collapse. In the week after the liberation one of the *hongs* did collapse, fortunately when no one was inside.

The internees described conditions in these Japanese jungle camps as terrible, almost unbearable. They also found it humiliating to have to live in conditions in which formerly only *koelies* lived, often without realising that it had been they themselves who had created such conditions. Any complaints to their captors about these conditions would have fallen on deaf ears. To the Japanese, it was nothing unusual to live in crowded conditions in flimsy dwellings and to have a meagre diet. They would not have minded humiliating the Europeans (and often did) but life in the camps did not seem to them to be an extraordinary hardship or humiliation.[24]

Sanitary facilities were next to non-existent. The latrines in both men's camps were just ditches that the men had to straddle to defecate. In due course small *atap* houses were built over the ditches for some privacy. The tram, as the latrines were always called, was a distance from the barracks, making it difficult if not impossible for patients weakened with dysentery to reach, especially at night in the pitch blackness with the only light coming from a wick floating in a tin of palm oil.

In both Si Rengo Rengo and Aek Pamienke, one of the greatest problems was the fact that every tropical downpour turned the grounds into pools of mud and slime. Rudy Kousbroek described the conditions well:[13]

> When it had rained heavily, and how it could rain in Si Rengo Rengo, then the path to the 'tram' was covered with a thick layer of red mud with the consistency of butter; you felt it squeezing up between your toes with every step and you had to be very careful to not lose your footing. And then you'd come with those mud-caked legs back into the *hong*, there was no water, you could not wash yourself; the only thing you could do was scrape off the mud as much as possible with a knife or a stick – and then you'd dive underneath your mosquito net again."

Those sleeping in the lower beds had a particularly hard time coping with what fell from above.

In addition to all this grime and dirt, infestation with lice and bedbugs made life especially miserable. Whenever the sun was out, the men used to haul their bedding and mosquito nets outside to rid them of these insects.

During early April 1945, all the boys more than ten years old were taken from their mothers and put into Si Rengo Rengo camp. For those who did not have a father or other relative in the camp, one separate *hong* was set up, with a number of adults as supervisors. Henk was one of those supervising *Hong* 8. His task was not just to make sure that the boys were all right but also to keep

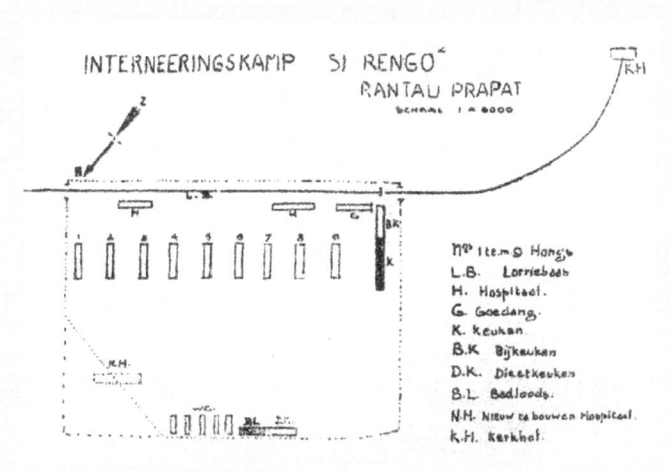

*Si Rengo Rengo camp. Hong 8 is second from the right.* [31]

them occupied, for boredom was one of the features of this camp. He still held quizzes and organised question-and-answer sessions – among his notes were pages full of trivia that he used for these activities. Less was done in the way of entertainment or education towards the end of the internment, for the energy of both boys and men was focussed only on finding enough to eat.

Many years later, one of the boys from *Hong* 8 – by then a pilot with KLM – recognised Henk on a holiday flight to Amsterdam. Capt Peng ten Velde had been eleven when he and his brother, who was two years older, were first interned with their mother and sister in the mountain camp Brastagi. Their father was Klaas ten Velde, who as an officer in the Dutch army under General Overakker was a prisoner of war. When the Japanese found out about the plans for Dutch leadership after the war, they tortured him to find out where the incriminating document was kept. In order to make it more difficult for him to resist, they had his sons brought over from the internment camp to witness this treatment. Peng did not describe details but simply said: "Those events in the life of a young boy can never be forgotten."

A fellow prisoner recounted in his diary: "Captain ten Velde was in a cage near us, a solitary cage. One evening he came by [back from interrogation] bleeding and staggering with misery, but when he saw us, he straightened his tortured back. What a guy!"[21]

In 1944, Captain ten Velde was among the POWs aboard the *Harukiku Maru* when it was sunk, and he died in the waves. The young ten Velde boys ended up in Si Rengo Rengo camp. Henk may have arranged for them to be in *Hong* 8, since their father had been his boss at Sipef.

Peng mentioned that he once had a rotten tooth that caused him intense pain. Henk gave him something for the pain – "some kind of distilled rice wine or *arak* which he still had stashed somewhere. He gave me some of it to drink and it really helped."

Peng said little in the way of smuggling went on in Si Rengo Rengo. Once in a while someone made contact with villagers in the plantations and bartered some jewellery for food, but it was rare. But he and one of his friends found another way to get some more food. "We were allowed to go bathing in the river, but my friend and I walked upriver, stark naked, to a deserted village where there were still some fruit trees and pepper bushes growing. We would gather all that was ripe and throw it in the river. Our mates were waiting at the wash place and watched carefully for our harvest, for the Japs allowed us to keep whatever floated down the river. We followed later, swimming the last bit underwater, and coming up just at the wash place."

No one would have noticed except for the fact that his friend, who had had polio, dragged one of his legs, and the Japs found his track in the sand, going in the wrong direction. They made him write a letter to his mother in the other camp, confessing that he had ventured out of the camp and telling her that he was going to be executed. "She never knew until after the liberation that this threat had not been carried out," said Peng.

The young boys were keen rat-catchers. Once they had caught a rat that turned out to have a nest of young. As they stood considering what to do with the tiny naked-pink blind creatures, Henk passed by and remarked that if they were fried to a crisp in hot oil, they could be eaten whole. It seems almost impossible that Henk, always a finicky eater, would even think of such a thing. A detainee's diary entry for 25 May 1945 seemed to corroborate this event:[25]

> The small boys are remarkably clever and independent; with their little hands they dig out the burrows of the many field mice and the other day I saw a few of them sitting around a fire with a small pan on three stones. In the pan they had boiling palm oil and each one in turn lowered a field mouse into it, holding it by the tail, eating them then with pleasure. This sort of extra food they really need. I heard that they also ate the cat of the Japanese commander.

In the last months in Si Rengo Rengo, people died daily from dysentery. This made such an impression on Henk that fifty years later, the mere mention of amoebic dysentery made him concerned.*

There was one *obat* that helped against dysentery – the new sulpha drug Dagénan. In the last year of the war, one pill of this miracle drug cost hundreds of guilders on the black market. For most dysentery patients, there was nothing available. Yet after the war large stores of this drug were found in Si Rengo Rengo, in one of the huts of the Japanese. That these were not used to save lives had to do with the fact that these were 'military stores' – not to be used for civilians.

Henk helped in the hospital, looking after the sick and dying. For him it

---

* When I was working in the tropics, I mentioned to my father on the phone that I had a bout of amoebic dysentery. I heard him gasp on the other end of the line and asked: "What's the matter?" to which he answered that in the camp this was a death sentence. I was able to reassure him that nowadays we had good medicines and it was no big deal, but it shows that the instinctive reaction was still there, even after all that time.

must have been quite an ordeal for he was a fastidious and fussy man – he hated messes and in later life never wanted to clean up anything at all. Nevertheless in the camp he took care of vomit, diarrhoea and corpses on a daily basis and without the benefit of soap. In later life he painted one scene that is quite unforgettable: together with another prisoner he was carrying a corpse out of the hospital to a hut where it had to be kept until the burial the next day. As usual the mud was deep and one of them slipped so that they tumbled all in a heap – Henk, his friend, and the dead man – and all they could do was laugh until the tears streamed down their cheeks.

The more desperate the food situation, the more desperate the risks the men were forced to take. In the last months when it became particularly bad, foraging was necessary. It was highly dangerous, as Henk described many years later: "We would creep out of the camp at night, under the wire, at a place where there were no guards. The guards would have shot us if they had seen us. Then we would swim across the river, which had crocodiles, and enter the jungle on the other side, where there were tigers. There we would spend all night searching for roots, fruits and leaves that we could carry back into the camp to provide the weakest of the men with extra food. When I think of it now, I cannot imagine how I dared to do that, but we did. We just had to."

Apparently there was another need that was filled by nocturnal excursions from the camp. From the texts at the Resistance Museum:[30]

> Camp Si Rengo was on a river and was fenced with barbed wire. Some men still got out of the camp. You could swim unnoticed from the latrines to the other side of the river. The men often sneaked away in the evenings and returned in the mornings. They brought us news about the war. Sometimes we also got news from the newspapers used to wrap food or objects. These were Malay papers, and they were read from cover to cover. Some of us recorded the news in a notebook.

*Post-war Allied photo of Si Rengo Rengo. Trees on the near river bank provided cover for the internees' clandestine jungle foraging excusions.*[31]

Among Henk's papers were a dozen or so lists of money collections that had been made among the men for the benefit of the camp bank. This money was used to order supplementary food whenever it was available. Henk, the accountant, kept the records. Each gave according to his means, some just one guilder, others twenty or even more. Receipts had to be made out for some amounts – possibly because the donor had contributed company money that he would have to account for after the war. The amounts gathered were considerable: on 25 March 1945 the collection was more than 250 guilders. As it was estimated that it cost about twenty-five cents to buy a day's rations for one person, this would have provided food for a thousand men for one day.

*Henk's list of contributions in Hong 8 for the camp fund.*

Officially the daily rations provided by the Japanese were two hundred grams of rice, one hundred grams of corn, seven grams of sugar, ten grams of salt, twenty grams of oil, ten grams of tea and forty grams of fish per person. What reached the men was consistently less: those who transported the food stole half the fish, ten to fifteen per cent of the rice and corn and a quarter of the rest. The fish that made it often arrived half-spoiled. At first the detainees were afraid to eat it, but in the end even stinking fish was consumed with head, tail and fins. No vegetables were provided and the rice-and-corn meals were extremely monotonous.

In this camp, there was no possibility of buying extra food from hawkers or obtaining any through smuggling, so soon the men were eating (and trading) rats, frogs, snakes, lizards and mice. Once in a while someone would catch a large turtle in the river and that provided a little extra protein. The *hongs* also took turns searching for edible bits on the garbage heap of the Japanese.

In October 1944, when a large amount of money arrived from the Dutch government, the camp leaders drew up a list of the items that were necessary for the camp – and found out that almost nothing on their list was available. It took months for some of the items (coconuts, vegetables) to come in. When stores did arrive, the camp was in party mood for days, enjoying increased rations and more variety. One of the diary writers recounted:[21]

We had a (very) small fried fish tonight. Not every one was lucky – there were only 800 fishes (for 2,000 persons). It was delicious. In the past an *hors d'oeuvre* of shellfish liver would have provided the same effect, and not even this effect. The appreciation of this miserable little fish, eaten in the pitch dark sitting on the mattress between the bedbugs was much greater.

Another poignant account was written by Henk Leffelaar[15]:

I remember that we used to get some fish in Si Rengo Rengo from time to time. It was fried in the camp kitchen and then distributed. There was never enough for the whole camp, so it was given in turn to two or three barracks. I can still recall how the food distributors fiddled trying to divide that fish in portions for their sections. In one of the barracks this was done by means of letter scales and even then quarrels broke out because one got too much head and the other too much tail. And this was about nothing more than a fish and a half, one finger long, per person.

The camp kitchen's fires required wood which had to be brought in from the jungle, where the men had to fell trees, cut up the wood and carry it to the camp. There was never a chance to let it dry so it was always difficult to get the fires going. As the situation deteriorated, fewer men were still strong enough to do the woodcutting duties and food had to be eaten partly raw.

The volume of the NSIO compilations that tells about the last days in Si Rengo Rengo contains a list of those who died in that camp. The last entry (number 116) is of a thirty-seven-year-old man who died on 15 September, a month after the Japanese capitulation. The cause of death? Hit by lightning!

*The hongs of Si Rengo Rengo.*[31]

## 15

# Turning Tides

**W**HEN THE MOVE of the men to the jungle camp was confirmed, it was bad news for the women. They didn't realize it was an indication that the Japanese were getting worried about the way the war was going. The camp commanders started to concentrate all North Sumatran detainees in one area south-east of Medan where it would be easier to control them, should the Allies invade.

October 12th [1944]
Today several women arrived from the St Jozefschool. Their husbands are all going to a new camp in Rantau Prapat, where we will also move after two months. It was a black day for our camp. They brought the news that a boat carrying the last prisoners of war was torpedoed and 150 men drowned. There were many husbands of women from our camp among them. We were all shattered!

It was a sad day anyway. We got no wood, so that we had to eat our food raw.

Another diary[21] gave a slightly different version of this event:

> To our surprise a number of women that were interned as families in the St Jozefschool arrived here. The Jap had not announced it. So we suddenly had to make space for them again. They brought sad tidings, a list of prisoners of war who died, the last of those that were in Gloegoer. The ship that was taking them to Malacca was torpedoed on the way. 105 men died, amongst them several of my acquaintances.... Everyone is down. These blows are hard to bear.

The ship must have been the *Harukiku Maru*, which was torpedoed in June 1944 by the Allies. Sad as it was, it was just one of many naval disasters that occurred in 1944. One account said that many 'hell ships' sailed the Pacific seas and were sunk during the last three years of the war but little is known about them. "After the war, investigators discovered that the Japanese had destroyed numerous records of these voyages. Between 1942 and 1945, it is recorded that 134 Japanese ships made 156 voyages carrying POWs. The number of prisoners came to 126,064 of which 21,039 died. Most of these ships were torpedoed by the Allies who had no way of knowing which ships in a convoy carried prisoners of war." According to Red Cross data, 10.5 per cent of all Allied prisoners of war died during transports by sea.

Rie continued to record the daily events in her diary.

> We have another duty now. We have to *tjangkol* and clean *parits* seven hours a day. I am still off duty for a week, because I still have those leg ulcers.
>
> Marijcke continues growing happily. She gains weight because of the pea soup we make of smuggled *katjang idjoe*. I keep selling towels and bed sheets to get enough food. From the Japs we get next to nothing now.

For a week we have not seen a drop of oil or fat in our food. We really hope that the end is near.

Marijcke is an ideal camp child, very easy and sweet, she has a wonderful imagination, can sit in her playpen and play for hours with her primitive toys.

**October 8th [1944]**
Marijcke is working on her second molar. She has dirty nappies and is very ashamed about that. At night she is very restless and kicks with her legs. Other than that she is very sweet and patient and hardly cries.

With Rie in bed with her leg ulcers, a girl from the camp took the baby for a walk every afternoon. The rumours about an imminent move kept coming. Rie hoped it would be a change for the better, with family internment. "I pray for that and hope for it intensely. In these difficult times you feel so completely alone. The more difficult it is, the lonelier you get. This life for us women is hardly a life any more. We are like hunted animals."

The food, she wrote, was getting less and less. "We are now eating the snails from the garden as supplementary food. Everyone is lacking vitamins and protein. Even Marijcke has a vitamin deficiency."*

A week later another smuggling event came to light, for which the entire camp was punished with two days without food.

A *soekarilla* was found to have eighty-five guilders with him and maintained that he had been given it by people in the camp. He pointed randomly at one of the houses, accidentally a smuggling house, where they found a sack of flour.

---

*My mother told me later that they were also eating the bark of trees by this time. Whenever I complained about being fat, she would chuckle and say: "No one could imagine that you were raised on slugs and tree bark."

Fortunately I was a meal ahead and the *nasi tim* was passed around on the sly, so that the first day was still bearable. On the second day, however, the Sunday, the Japs were on patrol very early throughout the camp. We could not make a fire. Marijcke had had diarrhoea all night long and cried with hunger. At my wits' end I wrapped her in a towel and carried her to the Jap and asked for food for her, but I had no success.

Banned from cooking, some did anyway, in secret. Several of the houses were caught out, and the women involved were hit in the face with full fists as punishment. "Somehow we managed to get through the day," Rie wrote. Tired out, they went to bed that night with legs weak from hunger. "I prayed fervently for food for the following day and fortunately this prayer was answered." After those two days without food, they felt as if they had been very sick.

A new camp director was appointed who seemed to be more respected by the Japanese command. Everyone hoped that better treatment would be the result.

**November 5th [1944]**
The new director has brought peace to the camp, fortunately. The Jap is behaving better and the women also. For a week Marijcke and I have been in a new room. It is a cheerful and sunny room on a quiet *kakilima*. We have both perked up. Marijcke walks around, lifting her feet high. I had bought some nice red shoes for her when she was born, but she has grown out of them already, her fat little feet overflow them on all sides. She runs like the wind. When she is sitting on my lap, she suddenly slides off and runs away. She is like a little wind-up doll.

When the children's milk was discontinued, Rie still had a tin of powdered milk which she opened. It was now becoming a race against time, "whether we will survive this, for we suffer quite a bit from hunger."

**November 27th [1944]**
Marijcke is becoming nicer and cosier by the day. She laughs all day and walks around on her sturdy little legs, and has all sorts of pretensions where food is concerned. She wants a piece of fish on every bite and since we only get a fish as large as my little finger every day or every few days, it is difficult to fulfil her wish! If there is nothing on her bite, she waves her hands and cries: *'tida, tida'*. If she sees a piece of fish, she laughs in triumph and takes the bite. She is a real little cat.

Her little girl even managed to have a real fight with the girl next door about the possession of a broom. Marijcke, yelling furiously, won.

On 10 December, Rie recorded in her diary that "many sad tidings" had reached the camp. Earlier it had been news about the loss of the ship and soldiers. "Today we heard that two of our best people have been shot by the Japs. Their wives and children are in our camp."

Some of the men who had been transported inland must have managed to contact their wives, for more details were surfacing about the new camp that was awaiting them. "Rumour has it that we will have to move to Rantau Prapat, where there is no water or electricity and the food situation and living conditions are very bad. But from Europe the news is good. We hope we will be saved more misery."

Meanwhile in the present camp the misery was increasing. Besides the daily *tjangkol* and carrying duties they now had to make rope for one hour a day, day after day, including Sundays. "I am dead-tired when I fall into bed each night," Rie wrote. "I have to help Marijcke very quickly. I have no time to spend with her. Please God, let there be an end to it soon."

The antics of the little girl were the only thing that brought some cheer: "The best game is to dress up. When she sits on the potty, she puts the lid on her head and that is really funny, she thinks."

On 15 December, all the boys ten years and older were put on a transport to the new men's camp at Si Rengo Rengo. The boys were excited but for the mothers it was hard to see their little ones go.

**December 23rd (1944)**

The past days were absolutely terrible. For four days the Jap harassed us with work. We were not allowed to spend time to do our laundry or clean our living space, but had to clean the camp all day long. That meant clean *parits*, *tjangkol*, weed and take away the garbage. I had to stand in the parits with my *koelie* wounds with the result that I have to rest now with a swollen leg and a horrible wound. Even the sick women had to leave their beds to do the weeding. Those miserable beasts! The excuse was that there were going to be important visitors. I did not believe it very much.

Then something totally unexpected happened:

...we were all utterly exhausted and close to despair. I had just returned from *tjangkol* duty when we heard the sound of heavy engines in the air. 'Is that the important visitor?' we thought. Some 50 airplanes were flying high above the clouds. All of a sudden I turned white as a sheet and started to cry – I felt that these were our friends. Another 50 appeared, the sirens started to go off and we heard bombs fall.

After three years finally a sign that we have not been forgotten. We were so happy. Please God that the liberation follows soon! It is getting so difficult for us, almost unbearable. All that dirt and no soap.

The lack of soap was one of the horrors of camp life for Rie. She later recalled that by this time a common *parit* plant was being used to make soap. She called it the *lidah buaya* (crocodile tongue) and indicated that this was the Sanseveria. In fact *lida buaya* was the Indonesian name of the somewhat similar looking Aloë vera plant. While the juice of the Sanseveria is beneficial in case of snake bites, and it is the Aloë that has the cleansing properties of soap.

Fortunately, her daughter still looked clean and fresh.

I take good care of that, although it is very difficult at times to keep everything clean. Oh, how Henk would enjoy her. She is so sweet, plays for hours with her building blocks. On top of her drinking mug she builds high towers and then she steps backwards a bit to admire her construction. If she finds a piece of cloth she winds it around her feet, because mammie wears such rags around her feet also.

Fits of childish temper were sometimes punished by a spanking, but that made only a fleeting impression on the baby.

As the end of another year approached, the Japanese command was changed once again.

**December 30th [1944]**
Almost a year gone, a year of weariness and sadness. We have suddenly been allocated a new commander who has discovered how we have been robbed of our food all these years. Instead of 90 grams of rice a day we now get 150 grams of corn, almost double the amount. We never used to get coffee although the staff in Medan always sent it. We don't have to carry such heavy loads any more, the oil and the bags of rice are now taken to the kitchen with the wagon again. We are getting papaya

regularly, an unprecedented luxury. Are they becoming a bit more humane now that the end is near?

Vitamin deficiency worsened Rie's condition, with holes appearing in her feet. The pain was incredible, causing her to cry like a baby at night. But her little girl loved her house arrest:

She was telling me stories the whole time from her playpen. For Christmas she got a new dress from me, made of blue voile, and it looks so sweet on her. Proud as a peacock she steps around. Her voice is changing. She is getting a low clear voice. After the bomb attack everything she says is about 'bom'.

Four weeks passed without a diary entry. There may have been little to report or Rie was too tired and depressed to get down to it.

When she took up the story again her daughter was no longer a baby, but toddled and talked:

January 28th [1945]
Marijcke is now 17 months old and as a real camp child she gathers wood as she walks in front of me. She picks up every piece of wood and every dried hard bean for me and runs to hand it to me. She does not want to walk holding hands any more. With her sturdy little legs she goes off alone. Every evening we have to visit two small babies. She is fascinated by them. She stamps her feet in a temper tantrum when it is time to leave.

These babies must have belonged to the ladies who arrived a while earlier from the St Jozefschool where they had been interned with their husbands. It is almost unbelievable that people would risk having a baby in those circumstances, but there was no way to avoid it apart from abstinence.

> Suddenly she has started to talk. When it is time to eat she cries: 'Ha, food!', papaya is called 'paya', the word 'potty' is a means to get out of the playpen. She then produces a tiny bit in the potty and then runs away, laughing loudly. 'Poekje' means drinking – something that she needs a lot. Other words that she says are: 'fish, ball, hand, wawa-woewoe-toetoe' the latter meaning car. She has never seen such a thing but she can hear them behind the *kawat*.
> In the evening she helps me clean the vegetables. Every little leaf goes into the pan. She is the sweetest little woman. I am so happy with her.

Rie still managed to see humour in the midst of misery. Putting her daughter onto the baby table in the night, she was about to stick the safety pins of the nappy into one of her furry toys "when that animal suddenly started to purr". It turned out to be a cat that had been sleeping on the table.

As the toddler developed, Rie was kept busy running after her all day and then recording her progress in the diary, for Henk to read at some time in the future.

> Marijcke is becoming quite independent. She gets her own water from the tap. She takes her mug from the table, goes to the tap that has a leak at the bottom where some water spouts from and she holds her mug there. Whenever porridge is being handed out, she herself takes the pan to the distribution point. She notices everything, a smart little devil.
> Her vocabulary has been extended with 'baby', 'auto' and 'pisang'.

Life in the camp ran on without much emotion. Now and then someone died of hunger oedema, with the symptoms of swollen belly and legs. The food remained terrible. Fortunately Rie managed to get a nice garden going and grew *ketimoen, bajem, kangkoen* and *terongs* plus tomatoes and beans.

That she managed to do this with all that other work going on, and with her poor legs, seems unbelievable.

> I prepare lots of vegetables that help to fill the stomach. This month we get 160 grams of rice, 45 grams of red flour and a small salted fish a day. That is all we get from the Jap. For this we have to do *tjangkol* duty all day, carry oil drums and bags of rice of 50 kilo, etc.
>
> In our free time we have to pluck cotton.

It would appear the regime of the nice commander didn't last long. To compound the situation, Rie wrote of "rumours about an exchange to Australia or deportation to a new camp where there is no water or electricity. What prospects! From our husbands we have not heard anything for a year."

Time obviously passed slowly in those terrible circumstances. Her last letter from Henk had been in May, only eight months earlier. What she and all the other wives dreaded was the arrival of a suitcase.

> When you are given a suitcase with clothing, it means that your husband is dead and already buried. Now and then such a thing arrives here.
>
> Anyway, we just wait patiently. There'll be a time when we'll get out of this, in whatever way, dead or alive.

Rie was losing heart. She had never been a great optimist and the unchanging bad conditions were wearing her down. In the first week of March, she wrote that everything continued in the same old way, "except that we have been given a new job to do." That job was making quilted blankets for one hour every day. She was still exhausted from a week of heavy *tjangkol* duties.

The main change in camp life was that death was now a constant companion.

> Two women in our block died this week. Many will follow. Everything is taken from us, we have barely enough to stay alive, we are aware of death every day. More and more people are dying. While they are still alive, people come around asking for planks for the coffin, for that too the Jap no longer provides. If you yourself do not take care of making a coffin, you are buried in a pig basket.
> I'll consider it a miracle of God if we get out of here alive.
> And yet, when I see our prospering and growing Marijcke, I trust that we will be among the living.

It was only the cheerful little daughter and her faith in God's care that kept Rie going. Her toddler was "getting sweeter and naughtier by the day". She was fighting with other children in the camp, stuck to her guns and had learned the phrase 'this is mine'.

> She has an infected finger from the wood gathering. She knows exactly what mom needs to be able to cook. All our furniture has disappeared as kindling into the *anglo* in the mean time. I am now chopping up my last little cabinet and after that I don't know what to do. God will provide for this as well. Until now He has helped us marvelously.

As if to contradict this expression of faith, the child's life was suddenly severely threatened:

**March 25th [1945]**

We've had difficult times. Marijcke had amoebic dysentery. She was so ill with it, one nappy after the other was full of blood and mucus. She did not want to eat for three days. I was so afraid that I was going to lose her. But thank God she has recovered again. Her test is negative now. Fortunately they still had the last of the *obat* in the clinic.

Rie remarked that with a sick child, she was more than ever aware of how difficult this life was. Not a crumb of soap to wash the dirty nappies. No light at night. Sometimes she had to change the child's bedding three or four times a night in pitch darkness. "The stool ran through the nappy onto the floor. I stepped in it and did not know where to put Marijcke. I was close to tears."

This was the only serious illness her daughter had during the whole internment. Undoubtedly the fact that Rie and the baby lived in a small room by themselves was the main reason that she had not come down with any other serious illnesses. Their isolation protected them from the many infectious diseases that were rampant in the overcrowded houses and *hongs*.

It could have been different. The baby book of another small child* described the early years of a girl who was interned with her mother, grandmother and three aunts in Java. At first they were relatively well off, living in houses and still allowed some freedom of movement, but later they were moved from one camp to the other, with conditions worsening all the time. Towards the end of the war, the women had forty-eight centimeters of living space each on the platforms in the barracks or rooms.

These crowded conditions caused diseases to spread easily. In the first three years of her life, that child suffered – besides common colds and ordinary runny tummies – a kidney infection, heat stroke, measles, whooping

---

* This was my friend Carien, a friend since kindergarten days.

*Marijcke, aged sixteen months.*

cough, malaria, chicken pox, an ear infection and bronchitis as well as bacillary dysentery.

Taking care of a sick child at night did not give an excuse for a rest in the daytime. Rie still did her share of the heavy duties, while the food situation was getting worse by the day.

> We are getting red flour again to eat and hardly any fish any more. Our food now consists of 105 grams of rice for the whole day and 75 grams of flour. For the fish we have to pay ourselves. The inconsistency of the Jap – we are not allowed to have any money and yet we have to see how we can lay our hands on some in order to pay for our food.
>
> It has now come to the point where I have no more soap to wash

myself. This is something terrible; this is the worst thing of all for me. This week it rained every morning. We are only allowed to cook between 11 a.m. and 2 p.m. and exactly during that time it poured. We were squatting outside trying to cook with wet wood, and mud splattering our faces. It is like hell. And you have to cook extra because the food from the Jap is not enough. This situation cries to Heaven.

And yet, there was the young girl, discovering the world. "All day long she cries: 'Mammie, look! Mammie, look!' She finds everything beautiful and wonderful. She is such a treasure and can play quietly with lots of imagination. She is like a ray of sunshine. I am so grateful that I have her."

## 16

# 'Buried Alive'

**June 1st [1945]**

Finally we have moved. For many years this was threatened and now it has finally happened. One morning 25 women had to come to the office where they were told that they would be interned as a family and that the other women had to move within three days.

We were shattered when we heard it. Our gardens in which we had *tjangkolled* with all our strength, the large areas with *oebi* and vegetables, in which we worked ourselves to death, we had to leave it all behind. Fortunately we were allowed to take all our *barang* with us, so that was okay.

We had some busy days packing and taking as much from the gardens as we could in addition to our normal daily duties. Our mattresses had to go the evening before, so one night we had to sleep on the stone floor. Fortunately I was able to get a playpen for Marijcke in which she could sleep that night.

It poured with rain the day on which our *barang* had to go. We had to carry everything to the station ourselves. I had two *koelie* wounds on my foot so that every step to the station with heavy trunks and suitcases was real torture. But never mind.

Worse days would follow. Marijcke had diarrhoea of course just then, the laundry wouldn't dry, I had to carry a pail full of dirty laundry.

That morning we had to get up at six o'clock Nippon time, that is 2.30am sun time. Since we had been unable to sleep we were happy to be active again. Marijcke was really sweet. Fortunately she was wide awake. I put warm clothes on her because of the wind. Carrying a backpack, a pail full of dirty laundry, with a potty dangling from the pail, food for the whole day, mosquito netting, blanket, pillow and a small case with clothing for the first days, we made our way to the station in the pitch dark. Marijcke held on to the pail with her little fists. We really looked like a couple of vagrants.

We were pushed into a dirty wagon for locals, everything in the dark. Thirty people in a compartment, together with chickens, cats and dogs. The trip was not too bad. It lasted 14 hours, but after three years of confinement there was so much to see in the world outside that it went very quickly.

The children behaved like angels. They did not cry, just looked with eyes wide with surprise at all the strange scenes that passed before them. The only problem was where to relieve ourselves. For the children it was quite simple. They sat on the potty and the contents were thrown out the window. For the older people it was more difficult. Now and then we were allowed to get out on a station and the women peed just like that on the platform, watched by Japs and *soekarillas*.

After a train ride of 12 hours we reached the final station. It took an hour before we were all standing on the platform with the children and the luggage. We had to be counted, as if we would have been able to escape in the jungle where they had brought us. And finally we were allowed to carry on. The small children and sick people were allowed to go on a truck, but suddenly there was again one of the 'friendly' friends who did not allow Marijcke to go on that truck. We had to walk 2 km to the camp along a pitch dark road with big holes, crossing bridges that were broken.*

I started off courageously with Marijcke on my arm, my *barang* in the other hand and a backpack on my back. After 10 minutes I could not hold Marijcke any longer and she slid down and started walking on her brave little legs: '*Tappe, tappe*, mammie,' she cried whenever we sat down exhausted on our *barang*. The Japs and *soekarillas* did not know the way to the camp so that we ended up on the wrong road and had to backtrack quite a long way. We were close to tears. Fortunately one of the young girls took my small suitcase from me, so that I could carry Marijcke, who started to stumble with fatigue. She promptly fell asleep in my arms.

In the end we reached the camp. There was no electricity. In the light of flares the barracks grinned at us, barracks made of *atap* with small low doors. In the dark we squeezed into the barracks where a plank platform was pointed out to us, on which we could find some space. And there we were.

The platforms will still full of dirt and wood splinters. We lit a few oil lamps and tried to clean a bit. We had no mattresses, so I put Marijcke on a pillow, where she continued sleeping. I lay down on the planks.

When Rie recalled that journey in later years, she would only talk about walking to the camp, how endless it seemed and how "*Tappe, tappe,* mammie!" kept her going. She said that when women fell and could not get up any more

---

* Later she also mentioned that the Japanese walked in front of them with flaming torches to keep wild animals away.

the Japs would beat them, or even kill them. It may not have happened exactly like that, but it was what the women feared.

An autobiographical novel written in 1947[12] contains a vivid account of this train trip.

> It's raining, a horrible constant drizzling rain. We stand crowded together, in silence, on the square, grouped by train car, seventy by seventy and answer with a simple 'yes' when our names are called.
>
> Quietly we shuffle through the gate. Our departure has to be as inconspicuous as possible. The rain-moistened rails shine into the endless distance. The small shops near the crossing barrier are all lit up with small oil lamps; how picturesque is the light on the few titbits!
>
> 'Like the old times.' A deep voice next to me sighs. A dreamy longing glows in her eyes. 'God, freedom, that wild, wonderful freedom!' It is there, behind the closed barriers....
>
> The rain drips. It drips on our strange clothing, our naked feet, the old soldiers' capes and burlap bags that some have pulled over their children for protection; on the stretchers with sick people. On our crazy folks: Mrs A that has loaded herself like a pack-mule, for fear that she will lose something of the last possessions; Mrs B who, guided by a nurse, gazes with deadened eyes down the railroad; Mrs C, deteriorated like an eighty year old, who carries nothing except an evening gown of a very special shade of blue, that she presses against her chest, her only luggage....
>
> When the train arrives we get in quickly, just to get out of that constantly dripping rain; to sit down finally. Small, narrow seats facing each other. Cars for *koelies*.
>
> The lanterns on the rails signal that the way is free. We collide, push each other, losing our balance and the trip to the secret unknown

destination has begun; the trip in a dark, armoured train through a night filled with rain has started.

Travelling in the tropical night. Like a cat who carries and drags its young in panic, the Jap is hauling us around. We ride, jolting and bumping on the narrow seats, seventy people in one car, between us on the floor the stretchers with the patients. Closed windows and heat and the odour of camp inmates that have not seen any soap for a year....

What an endless stretch and how endlessly boring! Coconut plantations, oil palm and rubber, hour after hour. In the cars the displaced are silenced. The children sleep, overtired, on the floor between the seats....

The rain stopped, the moon has appeared and showers a silvery sheen on everything, like in a fairy tale. You could enjoy it if you tried not to think beyond this moment.

Endlessly... oil palm and rubber, rubber and oil palm, just rarely a coconut or other plantation. Now a bridge across a brown foaming river, shining in the moonlight, then a dyke along large stretches of marshes. Now a bend where we hang out of the windows to see the blue blinking light at the end of the long train, then we're in a narrow pass through a hill and the locomotive is pulling the long train up the slope with moans and groans.

All the time our faces are lit by a rain of sparks, like a flight of fireflies, from the wood-burning locomotive....

We are standing on the small iron platform. Plantations and marshes, above which damp air hangs grey and impenetrable. Our conversation becomes less than optimistic. Disease and death, mosquitoes, malaria, marsh fevers and infection! Where are we going? To the end of the railroad, that much we know...

The clouds separate, the day breaks. No golden light, but a white mist that hangs over the marshes in the East. An almost surreal twilight. It fits this trip, this morning, just as the shower of sparks from the locomotive fitted the moonlit night and the sad rain fitted the departure from Gloegoer and Medan.

Naked broken trees without tops, half decayed in the surrounding marshes, tumble in the thin, surreal white morning light as the train speeds by. It is like a dream. A world of mists, demonic in its solitude, shot with grey morning vapours and overarched with the strange quiet, a strange deserted feeling....

Everywhere the children are waking up, start whining for food, for a pee. The cars are coming to life again....

Marshes, marshes, marshes. And then rubber again. The oil palm plantations are a thing of the past. And then finally Aek Pamienke! Mindlessly we read the sign. Aek Pamienke! Is this the end, so unexpectedly?

Look, there is our luggage, thrown in a large haphazard heap along the railroad. For this we slaved and hauled for days in the hottest hours to get it properly stowed into the cars. Our very last possessions!...

Aek Pamienke is nothing but a storage barn along the railway of the rubber plantations that lie behind....

Under the rubber trees that stand close to the railroad are a number of chairs. Here we sit down. They told us: 'Here we can rest and eat a bit.' We are surprised. Strange! How tolerant the Japanese are. Soon it turns out to be a mistake, as the group that has just stepped down from the last part of the train is being driven with swishing bamboo canes onto the road that enters the forest. Frightened we jump up; for fear of being hit many women start to walk, without a thought of where to. Children whine and cry loudly: 'Mammie, mammie...' They are exhausted. But they have to come along in the mass of mindless cattle that is being driven with bamboo canes and rifle butts.

'Hush... *djalan*... walk!'...

As we start on the plantation road, driven, loaded with backpacks and hand luggage, we get a glimpse over our shoulders of how the sick people are beaten with whips and bamboo canes onto the ambulance that is nothing more than a rattling wooden box behind an engine without hood.

THE CAMP CONSISTED of nine barracks, two wash places, three kitchens and four wells – "all this for 1,400 people," commented Rie in her diary. One well was to be used for laundry and dishes, as well as for bathing the children; one well was for the kitchen, for drinking water and for washing vegetables; one well was unusable as a rat and a potty with contents had been dropped into it. That left the final well to provide water for a thousand adults to bathe. The toilets, she noted, had not been completed. They were holes in the ground with a small *atap* enclosure around them. No lids for the holes, so that the flies

*Living and sleeping quarters in Aek Pamienke. (Joke Broekema)*[19]

*Daily life in the camp under the rubber trees. (Joke Broekema)*[19]

could happily hop from faeces onto food. The camp was in the middle of the jungle, completely separated from the outside world. "We are buried alive here," wrote Rie. "There is no light. We have to take care of that ourselves with home-made oil lamps, with of course a chance of fire. Here we'll learn to trust God implicitly, for we are threatened by a thousand dangers."

The camp had been constructed on the site of a rubber plantation which was surrounded by jungle. In a rubber plantation the undergrowth is cleared and the trees are planted in orderly rows. The bark on the tree trunks is light grey and the branches of the crown start at a height of three metres or more, making a light and airy wood reminiscent of poplar woods in Europe, or some stands of old birch. When the trees are being harvested, the not-unpleasant smell of the dripping latex lingers in the air. The breeze rustles the small leaves and can reach down to the ground, as can the sunshine. It was a much better atmosphere than thick jungle would have provided, where the air would have been hot and humid, the sun hidden by the thick canopy of giant trees, and the smell one of decay.

Many days of endless labour followed:

We should have had help from boys, the gentlemen had promised, but it turned out that we had to load all the *barang* from the *goedangs* onto lorries and that we had to drive these lorries back and forth ourselves. The rails were broken here and there, so that the lorries with trunks, suitcases and *tilams* fell over and we had to pull endlessly to get everything back on the rails again.

I had to leave Marijcke, who did not yet have a playpen, alone for hours. On damaged feet without shoes or slippers I trudged up and down the long road. Not much fun, those days.

All the time more people arrived, always at night in the pitch dark, sometimes in heavy tropical rains. Our hearts broke whenever we saw the exhausted women and children. The food is still insufficient. We are not getting any green vegetables any more. One after the other breaks down and gets symptoms of hunger oedema.

The work in the new camp was heavy, every other day *tjangkol* duty from 9.30am until 1.30pm. Much of the work involved carrying water. Rie recorded that the newest duty was digging toilets and that children as young as ten years were now expected to do their share of the work.

Rie ended up in the camp hospital, her legs in bad shape "with terrible *koelie* wounds". She had to have an incision made in one foot to drain the pus. The operation was "no fun at all", she wrote with typical understatement. "The knife was dull, so they tried with a pair or scissors, then again with the knife. All without anaesthesia." The pain kept her awake for many nights. *Obat* for sleeping was not available.

To add to her discomfort, she was sharing the hospital hut with four ladies who had gone insane in detention. "One of them gets terribly excited at night," she recorded.

The lack of medical supplies produced at least one inspired alternative solution. Mischa de Vreede, who was a young girl in the camp, described how they coped with the lack of bandages.[24]

> Even sheets were no longer available. Nearly everything was finished. The rubber trees around us provided a solution. With the latex you could do all sorts of things. You made a cut into the bark and let the white blood of the tree flow out. You let it dry and then pulled it from the bark. If you wound such a strip around a small stick, you had a fire starter. You could repair leaking pans with it. They did not become fireproof but at least they were waterproof. For bandaging wounds latex was used also. All you needed was a piece of material as large as the wound. Around the edges you stuck latex and that held it in place.

In the end, Rie was forced to stay in hospital for five weeks. Meanwhile, two of the insane people died, one with intense pain. "They were lying opposite me," she wrote. "It was not very cheery." Fortunately she had her little daughter's visits and antics to look forward to. Somehow, under those conditions, Rie managed to make a red check suit for her, commenting that "it makes her look fit to steal, with her blond curls."

> Every afternoon she comes to see me. She dances through life like a ray of sunshine. She has quite a temper and defends her right... If other children take something away from her, she hits them randomly.
> Once this week Harriet Liezenberg, who takes care of her, called her inside to eat. She always sits in a small chair with a pillow. First she took the pillow on her head and walked inside, then she ran back, hit Jaap Liezenberg who had sat down in her chair, out of it with a stick. Then she put the chair on her head and ran inside again. All this with an innocent cheerful expression on her face.

She came to me to bring me food. Suddenly it started to pour with rain, a real tropical downpour. Marijcke had to go home to eat. I saw her standing at the door considering what to do. She found a solution: she put the pan that she was holding upside down on her head and laughing out loud with fun she disappeared.

News had filtered into the camp of the German surrender on 4 May. "Could it be that there'll be an end to this misery finally?" wrote Rie. It was terrible, she commented, the way the women and many children were looking. Some were like stick people and others were swollen abnormally with hunger oedema. "They drag themselves around and still have to work and toil so much. On Sunday three people died, one of them being a playmate of Marijcke. Now Marijcke is the only child of her age that is still alive. God grant that I may keep her."

More deaths meant more graves to be dug and more coffins to be made by the detainees themselves. Mischa de Vreede noted that "on average there were one and a half funerals per week".

But then Aek Pamienke camp ran out of nails. "My mother used to walk through the *hongs* begging for nails for the coffins. In the end, when the self-made coffin stood in the self-dug grave, they removed all the nails they could still reach in order to use them again on the next occasion."[27]

The children seem to take it in their stride. One of the games they played all the time was 'funeral'. Rie and *tante* Harriet, who remained a lifelong friend, later recalled that because Marijcke was the smallest child in the camp, the other children always made her play the corpse, because then they did not need to dig such a large grave!

After weeks in hospital Rie was finally discharged. "I cannot walk very well yet and am not allowed to do heavy duties any more," she wrote. Her daughter meanwhile had become "a very independent young lady... She goes her own way, is very decisive and talks a mile a minute. The other day she was crying that she also wanted to 'carry *hong*' – that is to drag *barang* from the kitchen to the barracks. In the evening she thinks up all sorts of things to avoid going to bed: 'drink, bit of sugar, got to pee' – she has quite a repertoire."

When the child did finally go to bed, Rie was understandably annoyed when a noise or disturbance woke her up again. One such irritation was the *hong* leader's whistle. A woman who as a young girl lived in the same *hong* remembered the *hong* leader would blow a shrill whistle when she needed to make announcements – and with two hundred women and children making noise in the *hong*, that would certainly have been necessary. Rie's irritation with that whistle, which would either awaken or frighten her daughter, is the only indication that she was not immune to the stress that the continuous close contact with hundreds of other people could cause. Other diaries complained endlessly about this and the squalor of the living conditions. They gave an indication of the fighting and backbiting that was going on between the women all the time – about food, about space, about behaviour – but Rie's diary gave only a few hints at how bad life in the camp was.

> We have a new commander again. He has already knocked two barracks leaders unconscious. A very friendly gentleman.
>
> This week a list of deceased people arrived here from the men's camp. The Jap, who brought the list, told me casually that Jongbloed was *mati*. I felt faint, but fortunately someone else had told me just then that Henk was okay. It was another Jongbloed, fortunately.* What a terrible day, ninety men have become the victims of the shortage of *obat*.
>
> The days continue, we hear almost nothing. There are just VIPs visiting all the time.

---

* It was Simon Jongbloet who died of dysentery at the age of thirty-eight.

## 17

# A DOUBLE
# CELEBRATION

"There is a change in the air." Rie's diary entry was dated simply August. "All the time the Japs are promising all sorts of things. We don't ever get anything, but still." The camp commander warned them that there would probably be no more vegetables "because the trains were not coming any more. We cannot imagine ever getting out of here." Then...

> August 21st [1945]
>
> Another Jap came by, who promised us all sorts of things. We were given vaccinations, we don't have to do *tjangkol* duty any more. We are allowed outside to gather wood and look for vegetables. We suddenly received parcels from the men.

She recorded receiving a letter from Henk written in April, saying that he was all right. The letter did not survive, and with it went the many questions about his family and his reassurances for their future together that it might have contained.

There were more signs that the world had not forgotten that tens of thousands of people were living precarious lives in the internment camps. But still, in the camps themselves, no one had any idea that the war had been over for more than a week already...

On 23 August, eight days after the Japanese unconditional surrender, Rie wrote: "The Vatican in Rome has given us a terrific present. It was 13 guilders per person for which we are allowed to order food. There is something in the air!"

And finally came the day that everyone had hoped and prayed for throughout three and a half years of misery.

**August 24th [1945]**

This morning Mrs van Genderen was called to the Japanese commander. We don't have to do *tjangkol* duty any more. They promised us milk and coffee. We are terribly tense. The Japs that are walking around are excited and say that 'the war is over'!

At three o'clock there were suddenly shouts of joy. Mrs van Genderen and Klaasje Duim came back with orange [for the Dutch royal House of Orange] pinned on their chest. They walked proudly past the *soekarillas*. We can hardly believe it, but it's Peace, Peace! We are free people again. We sang *Het Wilhelmus* [the Dutch national anthem] like we have never sung it before. We all put on orange and ran around like headless chickens.

The idea that we don't have to be afraid for each other any more*, no more fear of the Japs and the *soekarillas*.

To be no longer harassed by those guys for all kinds of jobs. We

---

* This sentence is intriguing. In Dutch there is only one way to say 'afraid for' and 'afraid of'. I have translated it as 'afraid for' when it referred to the fellow inmates, because mention of treachery or nastiness between prisoners was rare – Rie mentioned treachery once but gave no details. Undoubtedly there was some of it about. Other diaries complained bitterly about the bitchiness of fellow internees, but in Rie's experience it obviously did not play a big role. So she likely meant no more fear of friends being hurt or killed.

thanked God that we got through this and we promised 'to remain your servant for all times'.

To quote a phrase from the national anthem underlined the great sense of pride mixed with the elation of the moment.

Not yet allowed to leave their camps, Rie and Henk made the most of the opportunities to communicate, as a letter from Henk showed. Undated and badly damaged, it survived among his camp papers. "My dearest darling," he wrote, "I am quickly penning this by the light of a miserable palm oil light." There had been earlier communication, obviously, for Henk referred to gifts that he had received.

> ...such good news from the two of you. You have no idea how grateful I am. I long so much to see you! Many thanks and kisses (you'll now be getting them with interest) for all the good gifts. So sweet, that curl of hair of our little girl. O, babe, to be free, what a wonderful thing. How cosy we'll be with the three of us. We should forget all cares as soon as possible.
>
> Be very careful, also with our little girl, in the remaining days or weeks. The visits are going, as you know, alphabetically and according to my calculations it would be my turn on Tuesday the 28th! It could be a day earlier or later, but it would be so great on her birthday! I am only very sorry that I don't have a nice present, neither for you, nor for her. I'll make up for it soon. Do you need anything? For instance, palm oil? I'll try to bring some *pisangs* and a few eggs. And I have half a bar of soap for you. And oh yes, I do have a surprise for the two of you, but that has to remain a surprise. I know you'll be very happy with it.

Henk arrived at Aek Pamienke on the day after his daughter's second birthday, with two chickens hanging from his neck on his bare chest. This may

*Marijcke at two: 'Those questioning serious eyes'.*

have been the surprise he referred to in his letter. He told Rie the vaccination made him feel lousy, so much so that he had to give up on the camp administration work he was doing. "Fever and headache. I always get sick from those injections. But that will be better by tomorrow."

He wrote that he was still one of the "strong bodies" of the camp, was fortunate never to have been ill and "although I still weigh the same as before the war, I eat next to nothing. Apparently I can live off the wind." Just as well, because "the monotony of the food is really terrible."

Throughout the internment years Henk's steady weight was a recurring theme in letters to his wife. It seemed that he was proud of it, but maybe it was his way of reassuring Rie that he was strong and capable, first to survive and now to take care of her.

His thoughts naturally turned to the future and making up for lost time with his family. "The drawing of Marijcke is great," he wrote. "Those questioning serious eyes. Now for some photographs soon."

"How will things be in Holland? Don't you look forward to going to Holland with her?"

With freedom beckoning, Henk was preparing his lists, organising the other plantation administrators and assistants to be prepared for the restructuring work that awaited them. A lot of administrative things were done at night for in the daytime the normal camp life went on with duties such as:

...being responsible for the boys' barracks. I am also the night watchman for the hospital and just for pleasure Aad and I are cutting wood (to keep in shape).

Last week Liezenberg, who is one of my best friends, said: 'Imagine that, with regard to the future, our wives can't stand each other.' And now she writes that you live together.

*The hospital hut at Si Rengo Rengo after the war. The barracks of 'healthy' detainees had two tiers of sleeping platforms.*[31]

Most likely we'll come together, that would be fun. Aad weighs more than me by five kilo.

Now, my dear, I am going to sleep in a very good mood. When shall we be able to fall asleep in each other's arms again? Another few weeks! Many kisses for you and Marijcke.

Bye darling, your Henk.

Rie's diary ended with her entry of 25 August. It did not mention the atomic bombs that had been dropped less than three weeks earlier, although she later recalled that they were told about it and that after her initial joy about the end of the war, she had soon realised that a bomb like that would have taken countless lives of innocent women and children.*

The men have come in groups to visit us. Sadly they still brought lots of bad news of men who died right at the end. Our joy was quite dampened by that.

Marijcke ran after everyone crying: 'I wanna see daddies.' She has already sat on many a male knee and loved it. At night she was so excited that she kept crying loudly through the barracks: 'To pappie, Jap gone! Jap duck, pappie sleep, mammie sleep!' She is adorable, the joy to be able to show her to pappie! He is coming on the 28th, Marijcke's second birthday. A double celebration. All suffering and sadness behind us. Now building together for a new future.

Other accounts contained lively descriptions of the reunions of the men

---

* She also told me once that at the beginning of August there was a day in the camp when the atmosphere was very strange. The birds had stopped singing, no insect noise was heard (and this can be deafening in the jungle); everyone was convinced something very important had happened but nobody knew what. She did not note it in the diary, so I am not sure that she remembered it correctly.

from Si Rengo Rengo and the women from Aek Pamieke. Ann Jacobs' book[12] was one of them:

> The second morning the men enter the camp again. With chickens hanging upside down by legs tied across bamboo, bunches of bananas, sticks of sugar cane. 'Tomorrow', someone shouts cheerfully: 'Tomorrow a lot more sugar cane is coming for all the kids.'
>
> We return the smiles, shake hands, nod. The miracles are overwhelming. There, among the others, walks a district clerk who had been thought long dead. We are so enthusiastic that some women jump the ditch to shake his hand; 'Hey, you are still alive!' However strange that may sound, it does not seem to surprise him. He only says, hurriedly: 'Yes, yes, I know, I know all about it. Where is my wife?' He shakes hands perfunctorily, looking around all the time. He wants to get on, go to his wife and children to tell them himself the good news that he survived.
>
> Little Marina, sitting on the rails, watched the anxious face of the man with wide eyes, then looks at her mother who has done nothing but laugh and cry for the last two days, more and more every day, more and more heartfelt, spontaneous. With intense earnest eyes she looks up at them both and asks: 'So are you my daddy?'
>
> 'No,' the mother denies and embraces the little girl. "Remember, think of the daddy in the picture,' whereupon a small friend pipes up:
>
> 'Oh, but I also have two, the one of the picture, that one we've had for a long time, and then that thin one that came yesterday.'
>
> Little Josephine adds, even more proudly: 'And my daddy has gone to heaven!'
>
> Then they sit together on the rails to continue watching the never-ending miracle, the daddies... the fairy tale...

When Henk finally arrived, he remained to help the women. From this camp he wrote to his family in the Netherlands. The letter is undated but must have been written around the middle of September 1945.

Dear all,

At last! At last! The first letter after so many years. And even this has to be done in haste. I hardly know where to start. I can't wait to hear from you. Hopefully you already received my telegram. The question that occupies my mind daily and has done for so long is: are we all still alive? Has mom survived this misery?

How wonderful it'll be when I can fly to Holland with Rie and Marijcke (our two-year old treasure of a daughter, whom I myself only saw for the first time two weeks ago). How grateful we should be to God when that rich moment will be given to us. The three of us are in perfect health and happy. After a difficult time of separate internment, prison, etc. finally peace!

As secretary of Sipef Medan, I have not been in military service. Within a few weeks we'll be going from this camp (a woman's camp where I have been allocated as 'strong man' to help). Then we have to start all over again (we have nothing any more) and we'll be coming to you as soon as possible!

Kisses and greetings to Mom, Annie and Carel, Piet and Miep, Karel and Rie, Puck and all the rest of the family, from Henk, Rie and Marijcke.

# 18

# THE AFTERMATH

It was 17 October 1945 before the Jongbloed family left the jungle camp, on the sixth transport, to go to another camp that had been created in a district of Medan called Polonia. There is a photo that must have been taken during the month that they were in the Polonia camp. It is the picture of Henk's dream come true: proudly showing off his daughter, sitting on his arm – the youngest survivor of all the North Sumatran internment camps.

In Medan they were quartered in houses, in very crowded conditions, and still not really free. This containment was necessary to protect them from the unwelcome attentions of bands of local young men who supported the newly created Republik Indonesia. The ex-internees had been so shut off from contact with the outside world that they were not aware of the dangerous situation that had developed in Indonesia as a result of anti-Dutch sentiment.

Even before the war, several political groups as well as some local tribes of the islands had started a movement to free themselves from Dutch colonial rule. Japan announced in September 1944 that not only Java but the entire archipelago would become independent. On 9 August 1945, the leaders of the independence movement – Soekarno, Hatta and Rajiman Wedjodiningrat –

*Henk and two-year-old Marijcke, 1945.*

met with the Japanese and were promised that Indonesian independence would be granted on 24 August. Eight days later, on 17 August, Soekarno jumped the gun and read a brief unilateral *Proklamasi*, the Declaration of Independence. On 18 August, the interim government of the Republik Indonesia was formed with Soekarno as president, Hatta as vice-president and the moderate Sjahrir as premier.

This government still did not have much authority. At first there were no police or army. This vacuum was quickly filled by troops of fanatic Indonesian nationalists, mainly untrained and undisciplined young men, called *pemoeda*.

They armed themselves with the weapons that the Japanese surrendered and that should have been taken by the British. These *pemoeda* created havoc in the cities and rural areas of both Sumatra and Java, murdering many Europeans and killing the British soldiers who were sent to stop their onslaught.

This gave rise to an odd situation: the Japanese guards of the camps now had to protect the people inside from the violence of these freedom fighters. Still, the Allies were slow to liberate the Dutch internees. Political motives influenced the liberation. The British especially were not unhappy to see Holland lose its colonies.

In middle-Java, where the new republic had strong support, the Allied troops landed only at the end of October 1945. Chaos had reigned in Soerabaja since 15 October. It was during this time that a number of the ex-prisoners of the internment camps were being evacuated with the help of a handful of troops from the British Indies (Mahratta). These Indian soldiers fought bravely to protect the women and children and paid for it with their lives – an act that went without recognition. The situation in Soerabaja was incredible: men from the poor areas of the city went berserk and tortured, maimed and killed every non-Indonesian they met – Europeans, Chinese, Arabs and even Japanese. The official Indonesian republican forces could not contain the rioting.

The Allies had not reckoned with such fierce fighting. Much of it could have been prevented if they had not dragged their feet liberating Java. Mountbatten, the Supreme Allied Commander South East Asia, kept his main force in Australia in order to give the Indonesians a chance to shake off the yoke of Dutch colonialism. It took the Allies until 13 November to capture the city, with desultory fighting continuing for another three weeks. In this battle, six thousand republican militants and six hundred British and Indian troops died. It is said that in these three chaotic months after the Japanese capitulation, more civilians died in Soerabaja than during the entire war.

When he heard about the events in East Java, Henk was deeply troubled. "The river was clogged with bodies and the water ran red with the blood of murdered people," he mentioned more than once in later years. He nurtured a strong hatred for Mountbatten. This hatred came to the surface when the latter fell victim to an IRA bomb in 1979. "He finally got his just deserts. I feel like raising the flag!" was Henk's comment when he heard about the assassination.

In Medan the situation was slightly better controlled. It allowed the repatriation of families to Holland to start by the end of September.

Soon the Jongbloed family had been assigned places on a ship. They had managed to retrieve some belongings that had been stored in the Sipef offices all those years. On the day before their departure, Marijcke came down with high fever and a rash. Because it was quite possibly a contagious disease, the family was not allowed to leave. During the delay the trunks with their last possessions were stolen from the harbour quays.*

The illness turned out to be, of all things, foot-and-mouth disease caused by the Coxsackie A virus. It must have been a very minor case of infection because by the middle of November they were well on their way to Holland.

In Singapore, Henk sent a telegram to his mother, after he had heard about the death of his eldest sister, Annie, in the Ravensbrück concentration camp:

Received verbal news. Condolences Annie. Will write soon. All three
perfectly healthy. Marijcke 2 years. Strength. Henk

In Ataka on the Red Sea, the penniless Dutch ex-internees were given warm clothes to be able to cope with the European winter. One of them, Rudy

---

* Although my parents always maintained that they had absolutely nothing left after this theft, some items must have been hidden elsewhere, because when I was searching for pictures for this book, I came across one (see page 41) that showed a small copper-studded Madurese chest in their pre-war home in Soerabaja. This chest has been mine since my teenage years.

Kousbroek[13], described Ataka as a tent encampment in the desert five miles from the harbour of Adabya, twenty miles south of Suez. Here the Dutch service that looked after the repatriation of Dutch citizens had set up a huge clothing warehouse. The passengers from the ship were taken in groups of three hundred by bus or train to the warehouse.

There were flags and a reception committee and even an orchestra (made up of Italian prisoners of war) that played cheerful music. Inside, there was a bar with free food and drinks that the ex-internees hardly dared to touch. After enjoying the refreshments, people were invited to collect a comprehensive set of warm clothing. Extra presents included reading material, chocolate, cigarettes and, for men, an extra shaving brush. Kousbroek ends his description with:

> Rarely in history was the end of an imperium introduced by a massive hand-out of underwear, berets and winter coats, to the sound of a cheerful orchestra.

Rie later reminisced how that evening Henk had put on his new blazer for dinner. As she sat across from him at the carefully set dinner table, she noticed a large oval label on each sleeve of the jacket. GIFT FROM CANADA it said – in huge red letters.

She also recounted another incident involving clothing. It was a day when she tried to put one of the new dresses on her daughter, but could not get the child's head through the narrow neck opening. The toddler threw a tantrum and was so furious that Rie, fed up and tired, put her out into the corridor to cool off. There she stood with the dress stuck above her eyes, howling like a banshee, when two soldiers found her, eased the dress into its proper position and calmed her with chocolates. Rie said she felt terribly ashamed, imagining how hard-hearted she must have seemed to these military men.

In Holland Henk learned more details about the deaths of his father (of pneumonia in 1939) and his sister in a German concentration camp. Annie, always his favourite sister, had been taken by the Germans because she had helped Jewish people by hiding them in her big house. After a short period in the Dutch camp Vught, she was transported to Ravensbrück, north of Berlin, where she succumbed to typhoid fever in January 1945.

For the year of their long-postponed home leave, they lived with Henk's widowed mother and youngest sister Puck in their Amsterdam apartment while Henk, still a Sipef employee, laid the groundwork for their return to Indonesia. That winter their daughter was introduced to snow and during the following summer to beaches. In September 1946, Henk and Rie's son Peter was born, an event that his sister announced to one and all in the tram after she had been to visit him in the hospital: "I have a baby brother and he drinks from my mother's neck."

## 19

# COMING HOME
# TO CHAOS

WHILE WE WERE recuperating in Holland, the East Indies were going through a terribly chaotic time that became known as the Bersiap period. *Bersiap*, meaning 'be ready', was the battle cry with which the followers of republican Soekarno fought for freedom from the yoke of Dutch colonialism.

The Dutch, realising their weak position during the year following the Japanese surrender, were initially disposed to negotiate with the republic for some form of commonwealth relationship between the archipelago and the Netherlands. The negotiations resulted in the British-brokered Linggajati Agreement, signed on 25 May 1947. The agreement provided for Dutch recognition of republican rule on Java and Sumatra, and the Netherlands-Indonesian Union under the Dutch crown, consisting of the Netherlands, the republic (initially only including the large western islands) and the eastern archipelago.

In spite of the guardedly optimistic attitude of the high officials in the Dutch government and army, the situation on the ground remained bad and became worse. Especially on Sumatra, there were many complications. Minority interest groups, led by the intellectuals of existing tribes, wanted to create independent states which they hoped would be given a place in the United States of Indonesia. They ignored the strong republican sentiment that ran throughout the population of the island, especially the young people. These *pemoeda* continued to lay waste the countryside, blockade the cities, and cause intense suffering to the people living in the *kampongs*. Since no one could till the land under these circumstances, hunger reigned and disease was rampant.

Republican leaders continued to stoke the fires of hatred against colonialism. Not everyone distinguished between the colonial system and the Dutch who were still present. Murderous attacks on plantation residences and workers' villages occurred throughout Sumatra. The local Chinese especially were persecuted and their homes and businesses torched. It was impossible to rebuild the country and undo the damage left by the war.

On 21 July 1947, the Dutch, claiming violations of the Linggajati Agreement, launched what was euphemistically called a 'police action' against the republic. Dutch troops (150,000 soldiers had been transported to Indonesia) managed to gain some control over the coastal cities and road system of Sumatra and East and West Java, confining the republicans in the Djogjakarta region of Central Java. After strong negative international reaction, the Renville Agreement (named for the United States Navy ship on which the negotiations were held) was ratified by both sides on 17 January 1948. It recognised temporary Dutch control of areas taken by the police action.

However, immediately after, the Dutch launched a second police action and captured Djogjakarta on 19 December 1948. Soekarno, Hatta and other republican leaders were arrested and exiled to Bangka, a remote island of the archipelago. Again, the international community reacted negatively, causing the Security Council of the fledgling UN to pass its Resolution 67 demanding the reinstatement of the republican government.

At a roundtable conference in mid-1949 in The Hague, the Dutch were

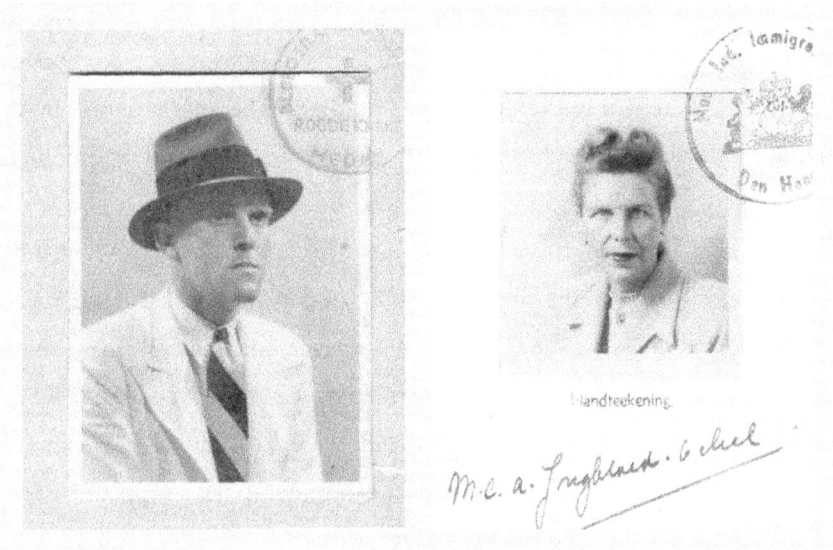

*Henk's Red Cross blood donor card and Rie's identity card, circa 1947.*

pressured into accepting a full transfer of authority in the archipelago to Indonesians. Although the Dutch government officially recognised Indonesian independence in 1949, the date of the *Proklamasi* (17 August 1945) has been recognised and celebrated as the true start of the republic since 2005.

WE RETURNED TO Medan in 1947. I wonder now that my father took a family with young children into the very unsafe and unpleasant situation that existed at that time, but I guess he went where there was work. He had been promoted to director of Sipef and faced the challenge of resurrecting the run-down plantations in an area full of murdering destructive rebels.

For the first year or so, we shared a house with several families. One of those was the family of Aad Liezenberg, the surgeon who had become my father's friend in the camp. My first memories stem from this time and place.

In the chaos that was prevalent in the city during this time, cattle often roamed the streets untended. My mother told us that she once even found a cow inside the house, rubbing itself against the sideboard. One day my brother and I were playing in the garden. He wore short red knickerbockers. A bull had strayed into the garden and apparently became annoyed by my brother's movements. It charged and stuck a horn straight into my brother's face, tearing through his upper jaw but just missing his eye.

Strangely enough, I don't remember this actual attack. What I do remember is sitting on the steps outside the surgery of *oom* Aad at the back of the house. Inside he was operating on Peter's face. After a long time he came out, looking exhausted. Timidly I asked him how Peter was. In reply, he hit me so hard that I flew across the back yard with the force of the blow. Apparently he thought I was to blame for the accident. He was very fond of my brother. I don't think he realised what he had done, and probably forgot it. I never did. I felt I had deserved it for letting something bad happen to my little brother even though there was no way in which I could have prevented it.

Like all Europeans, we used to enjoy relaxing at the beautiful Lake Toba in the Karo highlands. Weekends there around 1948 took some planning. The police action of the Dutch against the Indonesian republican freedom fighters was in full swing. Any travelling outside the cities had to be done in military convoy.

My mother told me that on one particular weekend, there were many Dutch soldiers on the beach, having an R&R break from the fighting. "We had given you a dime to buy some *katjang*." I remember the tasty roasted peanuts that you got when you cracked open the shell. There were usually two in a shell, but if you were lucky you might find three.

"You were gone all afternoon and until we finally found you, we were very worried. But there you were, walking along the beach with a small Indonesian boy trailing behind you. He carried a large tin of *katjang* and you were selling each shelled peanut for five cents to the Dutch soldiers. They all thought it was

*Lake Toba, circa 1948.*

very funny and gladly paid this cute blonde girl with business sense. In your pockets we found two guilders and some change and you had already paid for the large tin that your 'slave' was carrying. We were so embarrassed!"

But she laughed with a touch of pride. I don't remember that afternoon at all. It is strange how the memory retains some things and lets other pass through, for the weekend ended with an event that has stuck in my mind ever since.

My mother, who was never one to move quickly, had taken so long to get ready that we missed the convoy back to Medan. What I remember most is the extremely tense atmosphere in the car, with my father bent forward over the steering wheel, driving as fast as he could to catch up with the convoy. After some time we rounded a corner of the mountain road and my father hit the brakes. Just ahead, the cars of the convoy lay strewn like toys on and beside the road, some burning, some upside down. Bodies littered the roadsides. And there was silence, an ominous terrible silence, carried by the crackling of the flames of burning cars. We did not stop to look for survivors. That was too dangerous. The attack must have just happened and the enemy could still be close at hand. My father drove at breakneck speed around the hairpin curves to report the incident to the nearest police station.

Another time during the period of the police action, we were planning a weekend away from Medan at one of the Sipef plantations, Marbau-Zuid, where my 'uncle' Cees was manager – 'planter' as he was called in Dutch. I don't remember this incident myself but was told the story later. I liked *oom* Cees very much – he was jolly and seemed closer to us kids than adults normally were. My mother, my brother and I were going ahead with the chauffeur, while my father would follow later. For some reason we were so late leaving (did my mother dawdle again?) that we could not make the trip in one day, so we stayed overnight in a small *losmen* in a town on the way. Of course,

*Piano lesson at home, circa 1950.*

my father did not know this. When he got to the office the next morning, he was told that the plantation, where he supposed us all to be, had been attacked during the night and that Cees had been kidnapped. The two other Europeans, one a nephew of *oom* Cees, had been killed and – as it turned out later – fed to the dogs! My father must have been in a state of despair until he got the phone call from my mother telling him that we were safe.

*Oom* Cees spent four months as a prisoner of the rebels, dragged from one place to another in the jungle and living part of the time in tree houses. Later he told us: "I had climbed the ladder to this particular tree house and as I entered the room, the first thing that caught my eye was a huge portrait of Queen Wilhelmina, the ruler of the country they were fighting, hanging in a place of honour."

He had not been treated badly during his captivity but suffered hunger and dysentery. By the time his freedom was negotiated, he was a shadow of his former self. This change, this thinness impressed me greatly. Soon after his return he gave me a small gold bracelet with a little bell on it. "When you hear the bell you can always remember your uncle Cees," he said. I lost the bracelet long ago, but I have never forgotten *oom* Cees.

Whereas in the internment camp we had played 'funeral', now we played 'kidnap'. My dolls were the victims and often ended up decapitated.

WE CONTINUED TO live in Medan, where my father ran the Sipef office, my mother gave concerts and music lessons and my brother and I went to the Beatrix school.

I cannot compare our life in those years with the years before the war, but it is true that in those last years of the Dutch East Indies, colonial life no longer ran to the excesses that gave it a bad name. I don't think my parents ever saw themselves as oppressors anyway; more likely they considered themselves to be stewards in the biblical sense. We had four servants to help run our household and I never witnessed any problems with those relationships. Judging by the fact that they wrote to us for many years after we returned to Holland for good, they seemed to have been more like family members than employees.

Indonesia officially became an independent republic in November 1949. The post-war period of decolonisation, including the two police actions, had cost the lives of 6,200 Dutch soldiers and many, many more Indonesian freedom fighters.

We returned to Holland in 1953 – apparently in style. My brother saved and still has our first class papers for the passage on the MS *Willem Ruys*. But my father didn't remain long; he soon went back to work in Java for a Dutch company, owned by the Birnie family of Deventer, which ran tobacco plantations in Djember on East Java. He left us behind in Holland, living in the beautiful small villa that had been built for us in the woods near Deventer.

The time eventually came in 1957 for him to leave Indonesia for good when the Indonesian government first expelled Dutch nationals and then nationalised all Dutch companies. That was the end of his years in the tropics but he found a new job that took us all in the opposite direction: to Canada and a few years of cold winters.

When we once again came back to Holland in 1960, it was to stay. My father joined Philips where he rose through the ranks like a comet and after just two years was made director of a subsidiary called Splendor. He ran its lamp bulb factory in Nijmegen and it was during his tenure there that he was recognised in 1974 for his special type of social work by being awarded a knighthood in the Order of Orange Nassau. He stayed until his retirement in 1978.

My mother became very involved in various religious groups and found an outlet for her musical talents in directing choirs. And she gardened. It was a life-long passion. I was told that her garden in Indonesia had been so beautiful that the Sultan of Medan paid a special visit to admire it. From what I remember of our garden in Holland, she never lost her touch.

After a lifetime during which they saw and experienced more than most people could ever imagine, Henk and Rie died within three years of one another in the late 1990s.

As for my brother and me, Peter became a pilot, thereby fulfilling his father's dream. Now his own son has also earned his wings. I chose medicine and a life overseas. For me, Indonesia remained important. As a child, I longed for it all the time and when, in 1970, I had a chance as a newly graduated doctor to work in Java, I jumped at the opportunity. It felt like coming home.

A few years later I found myself in the United Arab Emirates, seduced by the attractions of the expatriate lifestyle and the warm climate, and there I was to remain for twenty years. I became involved in the conservation of wildlife and ultimately in creating the Arabian Leopard Trust, the first wildlife conservation NGO in the UAE.*

But all that too is starting to seem like a long time ago, especially viewed from the perspective of blissful retirement in the southwest of France. I've settled into it well. Here I discovered the truth in the French saying, *Le bonheur c'est l'équilibre* (happiness is the result of balance). That's what finally allowed me to sit down and write this story about two remarkable people and their will to survive.

---

* This story and others about my work with endangered species in Arabia are told in *Fat Legs Don't Matter*, published in 2010.

## 20

# AFTER EFFECTS

THE PHYSICAL AND mental suffering endured by the detainees over the years of internment could not help but have an impact on their later life. Much has been written about this; probably much more was locked away inside the minds of survivors: a chapter closed, over, finished.

My parents were not quite as reticent about their camp years as others were. I assume they had discussed their separate experiences extensively between themselves and thereby processed the trauma adequately. That did not come easily. My mother recalled later that, after the liberation, "of course, we who were still alive were happy to be reunited with our relatives, but we had all changed and it took a long time till we had really good contact with each other. Henk and I could walk for hours and hours without knowing what to say to each other. Many marriages failed at that time."

When I was growing up, 'the camp' was mentioned regularly, and as far as I can remember it was mainly in the context of food. It's easy to understand why, after the privations of camp life, there was never any food thrown out in our household. My mother became an expert in processing leftovers to the nth degree. I have learned from her in that respect.

One way in which my mother dealt with her camp experience was by denial. This became apparent to me twice in later years. Once, we were visiting a lady who had been a teenager in the camps. When my mother mentioned that those years had been a time of spiritual growth that she would not like to have missed, the lady cried out: "Well, not for me. Those Japs killed my mother and I hate them and shall never forgive them!" The other time was when a religious group had asked my mother to give a lecture about the internment. While she was preparing her talk, I offered her the baby book for reference, but she declined. When I read the text of that lecture, I was amazed. It sounded as if she had been in a rather strictly run vacation camp.

My father seemed, as always, more realistic about the camp experience. It had happened, it was over, that was it. He put those years behind him quickly and ended up working for more than a decade in Indonesia after the war. I think he would have stayed longer if he had been able to.

In the late 1960s, he had an ECG done and a scar was discovered that indicated a heart attack, suffered years before. He assumed that this was a result of the heavy tree chopping work in the camp. In the end, it was heart failure that caused his death, but he had made it to eighty-five by then.

My father's obsession about providing us with enough soap is almost certainly due to the camp experiences and indicates how important being clean was for him.

During the war and the internment, my parents were mature adults; I was an infant in her formative years. For me, after effects took some time to come to light. In her diary, my mother commented on my being an ideal camp child who never caused trouble. There was a down side to my being so good, but that did not show until much later when I seemed destined to be forever 'unlucky in love'. I had no idea what was happening and suffered frequent heartaches and depressive periods.

Then I heard about some research that linked growing up as a small child in the camps with a malfunction of aggression regulation. During a period of depression in the early 1980s, I wrote to Professor Jan Bastiaans who was an expert in its treatment. I described my problems and the circumstances of my early youth. His answer was that indeed it seemed like a clear case of deregulation of aggression, and he was ready to try treating me. But I was not ready then and never followed it up. I managed to deal with it in a different way later on. But I never did find a partner who I could live with, so motherhood passed me by, to my intense sadness.

The camps' appalling diet may be implicated in my lifelong struggle with weight control. Medical research has shown that starvation conditions during pregnancy may cause the lack of a certain weight-regulating hormone (leptin). This hormone and its effects were only discovered in 1994.

On the other hand, I may have inherited the very effective metabolism that kept my father's weight stable throughout the camp years. When a daily diet of a thousand calories is sufficient to maintain one's weight, this is a good thing during times of starvation but somewhat difficult to deal with in times of plenty.

It is certain that the lack of vitamin A in the camp food led to my night blindness. It does not bother me very much because, as with colour blindness, the sufferer does not miss what he does not know. I discovered my condition only later in life while visiting the night houses of zoos where I was never able to see anything of the exhibits that others seemed to distinguish with ease.

AFTER READING SO many diaries and so much documentation about the Japanese camps in Indonesia, I am led to conclude that the internment camps of North Sumatra, bad as they were, were not the worst. The high death rates of camps in the south, in Palembang and Muntok, indicate they were far worse. And although in Java people were not put into camps during the first year of the occupation, when they were, the conditions were intolerable, especially the overcrowding. In some camps, the prisoners only had forty-eight centimetres of space at their disposal, whereas my mother remembered the ninety centimetres of Aek Pamienke with horror. Even at the end, in Sumatra families were re-united (where possible) within weeks of the Japanese capitulation, and their liberation and repatriation were carried out much more quickly than on Java.

These facts combined with several others to contribute to my survival: first and foremost the dedication and self-sacrifice of my mother, who was able to breast-feed me for nine months and later shared her meagre ration; the fact that we spent the first two years in a separate room of our own, thus avoiding the crowded conditions in which disease spread like wildfire; possibly the low-metabolism gene of my father; and certainly the fact that the bombs of Hiroshima and Nagasaki fell when they did.

Another, more subtle effect of the camps influenced our post-war family life. My parents and I formed a *kongsi*; we were the survivors of a terrible time. For my brother, who had been born after the war, there was no place in this *kongsi*. I had occasional glimpses of this problem during my teenage years when my brother's frustration at being left out would suddenly surface. Usually he was introverted and we really had no idea what was going on. I did not figure out what was happening until after I had read my father's letters many years later and began to understand the mechanism of the *kongsi*.

There was no intention on the part of my parents or myself to shut my brother out. It was not that he was not loved. On the contrary, he was certainly my mother's favourite and my father was inordinately proud of him. From my father's letters, it is clear that he longed for another baby, a son. I certainly loved my brother from the day he was born. The closest I can come to describing what the difference was is to say that it had to do with trust. If push came to shove, you relied on the *kongsi*, not on anyone who hadn't been there.

Unlike many others who had been through similar trials, my parents never expressed any negative feelings towards the Japanese. They had both experienced that there were good men among them. My father had secretly been given extra food in prison by a Japanese guard. My mother told me that there was a Japanese guard in the Poeloe Brayan camp who sometimes came to play with me and told her how much he missed his own family. I think he was the one who gave my mother the egg that I would not eat. In any case, my feelings have always been very neutral.

This changed somewhat when, during the writing of this book, I came across war stories that showed that, besides cruelty of individual Japanese, there was also evidence of systematic, organised cruelty that is truly baffling.*

I have never had any desire to go to Japan, not even to visit the Hiroshima memorial site. My father's wish for a non-violent end to the war was not fulfilled, but it is beyond doubt that those atomic bombs saved our lives.

I thought I had no memories at all about the camp years. But while working on this book, I came across a description of Japanese uniforms, and suddenly I had a mental picture of two lower legs, clad in a kind of rubber socks, with a space for the big toes separated from the part for the other toes by a gap, like a mitten. The field of view was that which a two-year-old child would have. I searched through all my reference material to see if I might have seen a picture of this kind of footwear, but could find none. Then I asked a friend who had also been in the camps and she said: "Now that you mention it, yes, that is what the soldiers wore in Aek Pamienke."

I think my brain may have retained one single memory – of Japanese jungle boots!

* See Appendix A

## APPENDIX A: ENIGMATIC JAPANESE

THE BAD CONDITIONS that the Western prisoners suffered in the camps were not meant to be cruel, although many experienced them as such. To the Japanese, who were used to living on little food and in crowded conditions, they seemed normal, 'an inconvenience of war' as one camp commander put it.

Volumes have been written about Japanese behaviour in wartime toward their enemies, their captives and their own people. Despite much theorising, it remains an enigma to the Western mind. During the research for this book, I came across varied descriptions of the Japanese mentality, but in general and in retrospect, it seems that there was no intentional malice, or organised cruelty, such as was prevalent in the German extermination camps.

There were definitely camp commanders or *Kenpeitai* officers who had risen to the top because of their special ability to 'get things done by whatever means'. Some were infamous for their exploits (and some were suitably punished after the war). Many others just did their jobs, and the biggest problem in dealing with them was their almost proverbial fickleness.

In spite of the evidence that intentional cruelty was rare, it did occur. And when it did, it was extraordinary. In his accounts, journalist Bill McDougall[17] describes the slaughter of ship-wreck survivors on the beaches of Bangka, as told by Eric Germann, who was one of them. Their ship, the *Vyner-Brooke*, carrying 250 passengers, mostly women, children and old men, had been bombed. About seventy people, many in need of medical attention, made it to a small beach. After a night's rest, about half the group decided to take a trail leading inland, to get help for the severely wounded who were being taken care of by some of the men. While they were gone, a small Japanese contingent appeared. The Japanese ordered the men to line up and a machinegun was trained on them to prevent any escapes. Then they were bayoneted. Eric passed out. When he came to, the Japanese were shooting anyone who still showed signs of life. He played dead until they were finished and disappeared. When he was able to examine himself, he found that the bayonet had gone through his body without damaging any vital organs. After some rest, he managed to reach Muntok, where he found members of the group that had walked along the trail. They had met the same patrol who had executed his companions. Why had the first group been ignored and the second slaughtered? Unfathomable Japanese.

One of the worst of the incidents must be what became known as the Pig Basket Atrocity, of which I read several accounts; more than sixty eye-witness reports are said to be kept in the Dutch archives in The Hague. This was not an isolated case of cruelty, for the same behaviour occurred throughout 1942 and 1943 in Java and Sumatra. Captured soldiers were shoved into baskets of woven bamboo one metre long and about fifty centimetres in diameter that were normally used to transport pigs. The prisoners were often naked, although the several hundred Australians who suffered this fate kept their hats on and were thereby clearly identified. The Japanese had a special hatred for the Australians because they had put up stiff resistance in Java and because the attack on Australia had turned out to be unfeasible. Anyone who did not manage to crawl into the baskets quickly enough was stuck with bayonets. The baskets were loaded three layers deep onto trucks. Then convoys of four or five trucks were driven around the streets of villages and towns to show the local population what happened to conquered soldiers. The captives meanwhile were slowly dying of thirst, heat stroke and suffocation.

One Dutch administrator who witnessed this horrible sight in Soerabaja asked the Japanese guards if he could give the prisoners water. He was allowed to, as long as he did not speak with them. After he had poured mouthfuls of water from a coffee can in as many mouths as he could reach, he was beaten to death for his kindness by the Japanese guards.

The trucks headed for the harbours where the baskets were loaded on boats and then dumped into the sea. No one survived this execution. What is even more incredible is that this manner of killing was not just a method of dealing with military prisoners of war, despised because they had surrendered, but was also carried out on the elderly patients of a psychiatric hospital in West Java.

Sometimes reports on acts of cruelty are encountered in unexpected places, in books or on films. One such TV film is the recently released *The year 2602* – stories of children from the Japanese camps.[29] It contains harrowing stories, among them that of Simpy Vos.

Simpy was eleven when the Japanese occupation started. Soon he and his elder brother were moved to the men's camps where they had to fend for themselves. He said: "My brother was my all, my friend, my help, I relied on him." His brother had found out that there was a certain silver-coloured stone that interfered with the radio traffic of the Japanese if you rubbed it. He enjoyed this subtle (and minor) act of sabotage. But he was found out, possibly betrayed. The two brothers were taken by the Japanese and, with their hands tied behind their backs, hung by their armpits on a bamboo pole and left in the burning sun. After a long time, the Japanese gave them water to drink. They forced them to drink a lot and then told them: "When you pee you will be shot." The younger boy could not hold out for long. The Japanese did not carry out their threat but by the time the boys were released, the older boy had ruptured his bladder. He died two days later of the consequences.

During my two years of research, I was immersed in these and many other stories. It made me aware for the first time of the enormous extent of the misery that was caused in the Second World War. Even as I write this, a cold shiver runs down my back. Most Westerners, even the younger generations, are aware of the millions of people who suffered in Europe during that time. But few realise what happened in Korea, China, and the whole of South East Asia. Local civilian populations suffered unspeakable horrors even without internment. Hunger and poverty were omnipresent. I don't even want to forget the Japanese soldiers – young boys and men who had to leave their families, often for more than ten years, always on the go, never safe, never happy.

These things should never be forgotten.

## APPENDIX B: THE POETRY

**Henk Jongbloed**
*Voor Marijcke                Jes. 21: 12a*

Jij bent voor ons de morgenstond
Maar ach, het is nog nacht!
Hoe goed dat Hij je tot ons zond,
Bij Hem toch is de macht.

Je bent voor ons het zaad der Kerk.
Dat nimmer gaat teloren
Ondanks de oorlog groeit zijn werk
Hij zorgt reeds van tevoren

Je wieg staat wel in wereldgeweld
Maar je voetjes in de vrede
Bij hem zijn al de dagen geteld
Hij weet wanneer het leed is geleden.

Al is het nog donker om ons heen
Je brengt er de zon in ons leven!
Van alle vreugden is er geen
Waarvoor we jou ooit zouden geven.

Wie dacht dat jij nú komen zou
In een tijd van strijd en gevaar?
Wij steunen echter op Zijn trouw
Hij spare ons voor elkaar.

Wij zouden zo graag bij elkander zijn
maar 't is ons nog niet gegeven
Uw wensch, uw wil, 't is alles mijn
Ik geef u een nieuw leven.

Marijcke Victoria Désirée
In bitterheid ben je geboren
De zege breng je echter mee
en verlangensvervulling onzer
    dromen.

Eens kom je in een huisje
Waar alles Liefde heet
Je vindt daar óók een kruisje
Dat thans alleen God weet.

We zullen je steeds omringen
Met onze liefde en zorg
Jouw hartje zal steeds zingen
Dáárvoor zijn wij je borg.

Ons hart in kamp en kerker
Werkt thans al voor dien tijd
God maakt ons immer sterker
Zij het dan ook na strijd.

Geen wanklank zal er wezen,
Geen schijn of klatergoud
Hij heeft ons thans genezen
En 't huis voor ons gebouwd.

O kindje, zal jij begrijpen
Wat dit alles zegt?
Zal ook in jou eens rijpen
Wat in ons werd gelegd?

Wij zullen bidden en vragen
Of voor ons 'wensgezin'
De heilzon moge dagen
Alsook: een spoedig begin

**Henk Jongbloed**
*Marijcke....Zondag 12/9 '43*

Mijn lief klein kindje
Zeg eens, hoe vind je
Je nieuwe eigen bestaan:
Mijn kleine Marijcke
Wat lig je te kijken
Voel je je zo voldaan?

Wat wriemelen je knuistjes
Wat krabbelen die vuistjes
Heb je het zo druk?
Al die nieuwe dingen
Zijn ze niet om te zingen
Van blijdschap en geluk?

Wat is er, wat moet je
Wat trappelt je voetje?
Is je slaapje gestoord?
Zeg eens, wat uit je
Waarom dat geluidje
Dat de stilte doorboort?

Wat doe je toch, kleintje
Speel je begijntje
In je eigen bad?
Lik jij aan je handje
spat je over 't randje
Maak je alles nat?

God – Hij toch zond je -
plooide jouw mondje
is dit je eerste lach?
Jij bolrond snoetje
met een lach op je toetje
Schep jij vreugde in de dag?

Lig jij in je bedje
Te trappelen om een pretje
Of ben je heus kwaad?
Wil je nu al weer eten
Ben je dan vergeten
Dat het klokje nog niet slaat?

Mijn klein lief blondje
Waarom toch wond je
Jezelf zo op?
Nee, heus niet, dat weet je
Niemand vergeet je
Jij mensj'in de dop!

Niets zal je genaken
Zelfs zijn engelen waken
Ben je nu gerust?
Sluit je oogjes maar toe
Want je bent toch moe
Heb ik je nog niet gekust?

Je kijkertjes, wat zeggen ze nou,
Ben je zo blij met moeder's trouw,
Zorgt ze zo lief en zo goed?
Jij wiegekind, gelukskristal
Ook Zijn zorg staat eeuwig pal
God, die je ademen doet

Jij donzig, dartel diertje
Doe jij ons één pleziertje
Blij jij maar heel lang klein!
Genoeg van grote mensen
Die toch alleen maar wensen
Zichzelf het naast te zijn.

Jij allerliefst klein zusje
Je bent on liefdekusje
Dat leven heeft gekregen
Je brengt er de ware eenheid
En hebt ons bovenal verblijdt
Met hoop, geluk en zegen!

(Gedachten van verre en toch zo nabij
Ik zie haar wel niet en tòch maakt
  ze blij)

## Wachtwoord
*by Joannes Reddengius*

Dit zou ik willen zeggen
  tot wie jong
nog zijn en sterk en hunne
  zielskracht weten
oneindig rijk, die door hun
  wezen drong
en die hen dwingt met krachten
  zich te meten,
en wie dit zegt, het is een man,
  die zong
en 't rijke leven zingend schoon
  mocht heeten:
"Aanvaard het brood, dat eenzaam
  gij moet eten
den bekerdronk, bitter op
  uwe tong.
Wanneer van leed het zware
  duister valt,
wees moedig dan en ga met
  vasten tred
en zoek de sterren, fonk'lend in
  de nacht.
In 't woud van weedom nadert
  een gestalt
met hoog gelaat en milden mond
  en met
oogen, die weten en Hij geeft
  U kracht"

## Henk Jongbloed
*1943*

Voor U, Heer, is 't een wijle,
Voor mij 'lijk eeuwen, dat de spijlen
Mijn vrije wil de weg versperren.
Ik zie geen zon, ik zie geen sterren;
Ik zie slechts wanden, die zich neigen,
Ik leer zuchten, ik moet hijgen,
Van machteloosheid, onvermogen.
O, Heer, heb mededogen!
Zeg mij, wat kan ik nu verwachten;
Ik ben alléén met mijn gedachten.
Komt Gij toch tot mij nederdalen,
Spreekt toe mij in een and're tale;
Een tale, die ik niet versta
Die immer eindigt met: gena!
Ik wil niet uit genade leven,
Eigen kracht en eigen streven
Zijn voor mij het hoogste goed.
Niet Uw kruisdood, niet Uw bloed!
Geef, dat ik U bezitten moge,
Dat Uwe liefde niet gedoge
Mijn ontrouw van de vele jaren,
Die niets dan luisterschimmen waren.
Ik zocht, maar wilde toch niet vinden,
Ik liet mijn zelfzucht nimmer binden;
Ik vocht mijzelve maar omhoog,
Met slechts de wereld in het oog.
Het einde van het vele zwoegen,
Was altijd weer het aards genoegen.
Gij hebt van mijn cel een spiegel
  gemaakt,

Gij hebt mijn innerlijk geraakt.
Ik wist, dat 't eens zo ver moest
   komen,
Ik wist, dat tranen zouden stromen.
Ik wil mij nu gewonnen geven;
Slechts vraag ik voor mijn verder leven
Uw hulp en Uw geleide
Om sterk te zijn in't strijden.


**Fragmenten**
**Henk Jongbloed**

*December 31st 1943*
Uren, dagen, maanden, jaren,
van ruw geweld en oorlogswee.
Wilt Gij ons voor elkaar bewaren;
dat is deez avond onze beê.
\*\*\*

*January 1st 1944*
Wilt Gij nog eens een wónder werken?
Wilt Gij ons met Uw Geest versterken?
Wilt Gij de oorlog nu beënden?
Wilt Gij nog éénmaal uitkomst
   zenden?
Wilt Gij maken in ons sterk,
de liefde voor Uw heil'ge kerk?
Wilt Gij ons alle krachten geven,
om naar uw wil en wens te leven,
om na deze louterjaren,
Uw steun in 't leven te ervaren?!

**Zonder titel**
*van Rijnsdorp*
*gedicht overgeschreven in de brief*
   *nr.VII 30/1 1944*

Niet meer op verre bergen
Niet in een oude stad
Wilt Gij U eerbied vergen
Of offering van schat:
De heil'ge muren vielen
De bergen liggen stom,
Wie maar gelovig knielen
Zijn in Uw heligdom.

Wie maar Uw woorden spreken
In elke aardse staat
Zijn in de zuiv're streken
Waar Gij U vinden laat
Daar wordt op gouden schalen
Uit 's harten heil'gen schrijn
Gewierookt tot de zalen
Gans vol van reukwerk zijn.

Hoe zijn soms kort de nachten
Doorbracht in mijmerij!
Want op het onverwachte
Zijt Gij het meest nabij
Dan strenglen zich de handen
Ineen met sterke druk
En in de ogen branden
De tranen van geluk

**Fragmenten**
**Henk Jongbloed**

Ik weet het zijn uw scheps'len wel
Met hun gele zwavel vel
Linea recta uit de hel
\*\*\*

O, kom toch met Uw wonder
1000 dagen dit gedonder
\*\*\*

In een uithoek begraven
Zwoegen en slaven
\*\*\*

Ik haat ze met volkomen haat
Ik wens hun lijken op de straat
\*\*\*

Duizend nachten
...van vreemde machten
Die ons recht verkrachten
Waarin w'op uitkomst wachten
\*\*\*

Thans weer in advent
Temidden diepste duister
Komt Gij weer met Uw luister
\*\*\*

's Morgens komt de duisternis
's middags, elk moment
Als ik jou niet zie
Die mijn daglicht bent
\*\*\*

Ik heb aan een golf een dwaze
   vraag gedaan
Hebt gij een eigen wezen en bestaan?
Zij sprak: zie toch mijn fiere
   hoge pluim
Mijn slanke welving en mijn kroon
   van schuim,
Zie hoe ik trots ten wijde hemel streef
Ik ben alleen mijzelve want ik leef
Toen zeeg zij in de waat'ren met
   een zucht
Er was wat schuim slechts en een
   diep gerucht
\*\*\*

Is het als de wolken
Maan en sterren keet'nen
in hun zwarte kolken
Is het als de zomer gaat
En de laatste roos
Haar kleur moede vallen laat?
Is het als de zon
Achter verre heuvels daalt
En de nacht begon?

Nee, dat zijn maar schaduwen
\*\*\*

De aanval met de bajonet
Wordt nuchter, zaak'lijk ingezet.
Het ware handwerk van de strijd
Eist discipline, koel beleid.
Daar gaan ze dan, de vele horden,
De stelling moet genomen worden.
Van 't ene graf in 't and're graf,
Niet aarzelen, alles op een draf!
Een kogelregen fluit in 't ronde
Ze vallen met vertrokken monden
Voort! Je prooi is nu in 't zicht
Vage contouren in 't schemerlicht.
Klaar voor de donkerste der nachten
Waarin de mens de mens gaat
  slachten.
Kloppende harten, verbijsterde zinnen,
Nu gaat de dodendans beginnen!
Ied're steek een kruis
Ied're steek weer rouw in huis..
Een laatste blik, een laatste wens,
Het einde van de oorlogsmens!
Niet dralen, steek maar toe,
Voor het jou een ander doe!
Ied're steek een nieuwe dode
Ied're steek een rauwe, rode
Wond, die nimmer zal genezen
In huis zal 't voortaan stiller wezen.
Jong leven gaat....

**Henk Jongbloed**
*31 Dec. '44 (kamp: Si Rengo Rengo,*
  *genaamd 'de Doden Vallei'*

Wat houdt ge d'toekomst ons
  veborgen,
Wat dekt uw somber wolk gordijn;
Is 't avond thans of is het morgen,
Zal 't licht of zal het donker zijn?

De vraag, die ons thans bezig houdt
Waarop geen antwoord is te geven;
Doch hij, die op God alleen vertrouwt,
Zal ook in 't donker lichtend leven.

Hij leeft gerust van dag tot dag,
Hij blijft niet bij zijn zorgen;
Want in zijn ziele is de lach
Van de bevrijdingsmorgen!
\*\*\*

Wij willen op U wachten, Heer,
Wij, van elkaar gescheiden,
Die zeker weten, beiden,
Dat Gij 't getij zult keren.

Leer ons geduld, verdraagzaamheid,
Zo lang het nog moet duren;
De dagen worden slechts tot uren,
Als Gij maar heel dicht bij ons zijt.

## GLOSSARY OF INDONESIAN WORDS

(*Italised words are Japanese*)

| | |
|---|---|
| anglo | small wrought iron stove |
| apa kabar | how are you? – literally 'what is the news' |
| atap | palm leaf construction material |
| bajem, kangkoen | types of spinach |
| balé-balé | bamboo bench |
| barang | belongings, luggage |
| bersiap | 'be prepared' |
| djemoer | to dry in the sun |
| djeroek | citrus fruit |
| gedek | panels woven of split bamboo strips, also the fence around the camps |
| gedekken | smuggling across the fence |
| goedang | shed, storeroom |
| gula djawa | palm sugar pressed in rolls |
| *hantjo* | camp commander |
| hong | large godown, barracks |
| ikan teri | tiny salted dried fishes |
| kabar angin | grapevine (lit. 'news of the wind') |
| kabar baik | I am well, literally 'the news is good' |
| kain | piece of cloth |

# Glossary

| | |
|---|---|
| kaki lima | lit. 'five foot' – an appr. five foot wide covered corridor along the living quarters |
| kampong | village of local housing, made of bamboo, sometimes within urban areas |
| kasian | pity |
| katjang | peanuts |
| katjang idjoe | mung beans |
| kawat | enclosure, fence |
| ketimoen | cucumber |
| koelie | labourer |
| koening | turmeric (lit. 'yellow') |
| kongsi | group of people with common interests |
| krakat | vegetable |
| kretek | clove cigarette |
| kumpulan | meeting |
| lakoe | popular |
| larong | flying termite |
| losmen | lodgement, small hotel |
| mati | dead |
| nasi | rice |
| nasi tim | soft rice porridge with vegetables and sometimes a little meat |
| obat | medicine |
| oebi (ramboet) | sweet potato |
| oebi kajoe | cassave |
| pantjoeran | bathing area |
| papaya | pawpaw |

| | |
|---|---|
| parit | ditch |
| pasar | market |
| pisang | banana |
| rampok | rob and steal |
| *romusha* | forced labourer |
| sado | horse drawn cart |
| saja | I, yes |
| sapoe (lidi) | broom made of the central nerves of palm leaves |
| sarong | cotton wrap |
| *soekarilla, soekarella* | volunteer local soldier |
| tempat | place |
| terong | aubergine |
| tida | no |
| tidoer | sleep |
| tilam | mattress |
| tjangkol | pick-axe, to work the land with a pick-axe |

## SOURCES AND SELECTED BIBLIOGRAPHY

1. Beets, N. *De verre oorlog*, 1982, ISBN 90 6009 486 7
2. Bekkering P.G.and M. *De Japanse kampen: nog geen verleden tijd*, NTvG 124, nr 13, 1980
3. Burki, C. *Achter de Kawat*, 1979, ISBN 90 5064 314 3
4. Colijn, H. *De kracht van een lied*, 1989, ISBN 90 5194 024 6
5. Elias, W.H.J. *De Japanse bezetting van Nederland-Indië*, ISBN 90 6122 6597
6. Grendel, A.L. *Gekooide vogel*, 1995, 1976, ISBN 90 5194 120 X
7. Fergusson, M. *Mammie, ik ga dood*, ISBN 90 258 0428 4
8. Helfferich-Koch, H. *Een dal in Ambarawa*, 1981, ISBN 89 218 2871 5
9. Hillen, E. *The way of a boy*, 1993, ISBN 0 670 85049 7
10. Hofstra Layson, A. *Lost Childhood*, 2008, ISBN 978-1-4253-0321-0
11. Hollander, I. *Silenced Voices*, 2008, ISBN 978-0-89680-269-8
12. Jacobs, A. *Ontwortelden*, 1947.
13. Kousbroek, R. *Terug naar Negri Pan Erkoms*, 1995, ISBN 90 290 4801 8
14. Kousbroek, R. *Het Oost-Indisch kamp syndroom*, 1992, ISBN 90 290 1891 7
15. Leffelaar, H.L. *De Japanse regeering betaalt aan toonder*, 1980, ISBN 90 218 1909 6
16. Manders, J. *De Lach uit Leed geboren*, no data.
17. McDougall Jr., W.H. *Six Bells Off Java & By Eastern Windows*, 1983, ISBN 0-914740-27-X
18. Milton, G. *Nathaniel's Nutmeg*, ISBN 0 340 69676 1.

19. Museon, The Hague
20. Schoonenberg, B. *De poorten der hel*, 1978, ISBN 90 269 45485
21. Stichting Noord Sumatra documentatie *Noord Sumatra in Oorlogstijd*, 1991 - 1995
22. Takeyama, M. *Harp of Burma*, 1966, ISBN 0-8084-0232-7
23. Van Eijk-van Velzen, T. *Vrouwen op Sumatra – achter Japans prikkeldraad*, 1983
24. Van Velden, D. *De Japanse burgerkampen*, 1977, ISBN 90 6135 241
25. Van de Velde, J.J. *Brieven uit Sumatra*, 1982, ISBN 90 6135 325 4
26. Vervoort, H. *Kind van de Oost*, 2005, ISBN 90 388 7437 5
27. de Vreede, M. *Een hachelijk bestaan*, 1974, ISBN 90 234 0475 0
28. Zwaan, J. *Nederlands-Indië 1940-1946 vol. III*, 1985, ISBN 90 6707 083 1
29. Documentary: *The year 2602, The war that did not end* (Stories of children from the Japanese camps)

**Websites:**
30. www.verzetsmuseum.org
31. www.rouveroy.com

www.ingramcontent.com/pod-product-compliance
Lightning Source LLC
LaVergne TN
LVHW041611070426
835507LV00008B/195